D1140552

THE WORLD'S GREATEST BOOK OF USELESS INFORMATION

THE WORLD'S GREATEST BOOK OF USELESS INFORMATION

BY NOEL BOTHAM

JOHN BLAKE

Published by John Blake Publishing Ltd,
3, Bramber Court, 2 Bramber Road,
London W14 9PB, England

www.blake.co.uk

First published in hardback in 2004

ISBN 1 84454 069 3

All rights reserved. No part of this publication may be reproduced, stored in a
retrieval system, or in any form or by any means, without the prior permission in
writing of the publisher, nor be otherwise circulated in any form of binding or cover
other than that in which it is published and without a similar condition including
this condition being imposed on the subsequent publisher.

British Library Cataloguing-in-Publication Data:

A catalogue record for this book is available from the British Library.

Design by www.envydesign.co.uk

Printed in Great Britain by CPD, Wales

3 5 7 9 10 8 6 4

© Text copyright Noel Botham 2004

Papers used by John Blake Publishing are natural, recyclable products made from
wood grown in sustainable forests. The manufacturing processes conform to the
environmental regulations of the country of origin.

Every attempt has been made to contact the relevant copyright-holders, but some
were unobtainable. We would be grateful if the appropriate people could contact us.

As always, to Lesley Lewis
for her love and encouragement

CONTENTS

1

ARTS AND ENTERTAINMENT

ARTS AND ENTERTAINMENT

- When Marlon Brando signs into hotels, he goes under the name Lord Greystoke, aka Tarzan.

- Batman actor Michael Keaton's real name is Michael Douglas.

- The largest number of fatalities on a film set is 40, occurring during the making of *The Sword of Tipu Sultan* (1989).

- Norma Talmadge made the first footprints in the Hollywood Walk of Fame outside Grauman's Chinese Theater in May 1927.

- *Some Like it Hot* (1959) was originally called *Not Tonight, Josephine*.

- One of the actors in *Reservoir Dogs* (1992), Eddie Bunker (Mr Blue), was a real former criminal and was once on the FBI's Ten Most Wanted list.

- Screen 6 at Atlanta's CNN Center has been showing *Gone with the Wind* twice a day, 365 times a year since the film's release in 1939.

- Dirk Bogarde's real name is Derek Jules Gaspard Ulric Niven van den Bogaerde.

——— ARTS AND ENTERTAINMENT ———

- In 1944, Barry Fitzgerald got an Oscar nomination in both the Best Actor and Best Supporting Actor categories for the same role in *Going My Way*.

- The first ever Academy Awards ceremony lasted five minutes, with tickets costing just $10.

- In *Zulu* (1964), some of the Zulu warriors are blatantly wearing the wrist-watches they were paid with.

- Disney's *Beauty and the Beast* (1991) is the only animated film ever to be nominated for a Best Picture Oscar.

- Judy Garland was 17 years old when she appeared in *The Wizard of Oz*.

- Michael Caine, Sean Connery, Steve McQueen, Cher and Tom Cruise never finished school.

- Brad Pitt once worked as a chicken for the El Pollo Loco restaurant chain.

- Marni Nixon provided the singing voice for Audrey Hepburn's character in *My Fair Lady* (1964).

- Elizabeth Taylor and Richard Burton first married in Canada in 1964, and then again in Botswana in 1975.

ARTS AND ENTERTAINMENT

- The first film to show the sex act was *Extase* in 1932.

- The longest ever interval between an original film and its sequel is 46 years – between *The Wizard of Oz* and *Return to Oz*.

- Since 1989, to avoid offending losers, Oscar presenters say, 'And the Oscar goes to…' instead of 'And the winner is…'.

- Darth Vader has advertised Duracell batteries.

- *Star Wars* was originally called *The Adventures of Luke Starkiller*. The hero's name was later changed from Starkiller to Skywalker for fear that it was too violent.

- The first ever remake was the 1904 re-release of *The Great Train Robbery* (1903).

- A record 8,552 animals were featured in *Around the World in Eighty Days* (1956).

- In 1925, MGM ran a contest to find a new name for Lucille Le Sueur. They settled on Joan Crawford.

- The shortest ever Hollywood marriage is the six-hour union of Rudolph Valentino and Jean Acker.

——— ARTS AND ENTERTAINMENT ———

- Laurence Olivier is the only actor to direct himself in an Oscar-winning performance – in *Hamlet* (1948).

- The only soundtrack to outgross the movie is *Superfly* (1972).

- Paul Newman is the joint owner of an Indy car racing team.

- Charlie Chaplin first spoke on film in *The Great Dictator* (1940).

- James Dean recorded an album called *Jungle Rhythm*.

- Oliver Reed was once a bouncer for a strip club.

- Roger Moore is the only English actor to have played the role of James Bond. Sean Connery is Scottish, George Lazenby is Australian, Timothy Dalton is Welsh and Pierce Brosnan is Irish.

- The Hitchcock film *North by Northwest* (1959) takes its name from a *Hamlet* quote: 'I am but mad north-northwest.'

- Elizabeth Hurley checks into hotels under the name Rebecca de Winter.

———— ARTS AND ENTERTAINMENT ————

- *Braveheart* (1995) director/producer Mel Gibson was investigated by RSPCA inspectors, who refused to believe the horses on show weren't real but mechanical.

- On the set of *The Usual Suspects* (1995), Kevin Spacey glued his fingers together to keep his left hand consistently paralysed.

- An Oscar statuette is 34.3 cm tall.

- Jane Seymour's real name is Joyce Penelope Wilhelmina Frankenberg.

- Hollywood actor Tony Curtis is great friends with Harrods owner Mohammed Al Fayed.

- The Roosevelt Hotel, in Hollywood, is apparently haunted by the ghost of Marilyn Monroe.

- Thora Birch, the actress who played Janie in *American Beauty* (1999), was only 17 during filming and so her nude scene had to be filmed in the presence of her parents and child labour representatives.

- Doris Day's dog was named after the beer Heineken.

- The Oscar award ceremony has never been cancelled.

———— ARTS AND ENTERTAINMENT ————

- Both Richard Burton and Peter O'Toole have been Oscar nominated a record seven times without winning.

- Disney Studios has the record for the biggest global box-office year of all time, grossing over $3 billion in 2003.

- 29 August 1997 is the Judgement Day from *Terminator 2* (1991).

- The *Braveheart* sword was auctioned in New York in 2001 for $135,000.

- *The Wizard of Oz* (1939) was released in England with an X certificate.

- MGM's Irving Thalberg rejected *Gone with the Wind*, saying 'No Civil War picture ever made a nickel!'

- As a prop, ET was insured for $1.3 million.

- In *Star Wars* when the storm troopers break into the control room where R2-D2 and C-3PO are hiding, one of them smacks his head on the door and falls backwards.

- In 1977, one in 20 American film-goers saw *Star Wars* more than once.

──── ARTS AND ENTERTAINMENT ────

- Actor Henry Winkler, aka the Fonz in US TV series *Happy Days*, was considered for the part of Danny Zuko in *Grease* (1978).

- MGM had a reputation for being the most glamorous film studio, based on its having white telephones.

- Comedian, director, actor and author Billy Crystal has won three Emmy awards for hosting the Oscars.

- In the 1959 film *Ben-Hur*, nine chariots start the chariot race, but six crash and four finish, making a total of ten.

- In *Casablanca* (1942), Humphrey Bogart adlibbed the line 'Here's looking at you, kid.'

- The company names responsible for the end of the world in the *Terminator* movies, Skynet and Cyberdyne Systems, actually exist.

- In *Gladiator* (2000), during the battle with the Barbarian Horde one of the chariots is turned over, revealing a gas cylinder in the back.

- The roar of the T-Rex in *Jurassic Park* (1993) is a blast from a baby elephant mixed with alligator growls and tiger shrieks.

ARTS AND ENTERTAINMENT

- Robert Duvall's character in *Apocalypse Now* (1979), Colonel Kilgore, was originally called Colonel Kharnage.

- Bob Hope hosted the Academy Awards a record 16 times.

- As well as the handprints and footprints outside Grauman's Chinese Theater in Hollywood, you'll also find casts of Groucho Marx's cigar, Betty Grable's legs, Jimmy Durante's nose, Trigger's hooves, Harold Lloyd's glasses and Whoopi Goldberg's braids.

- Between 1990 and 1995, Holocaust films won four out of five Best Documentary Oscars.

- The Hollywood sign originally read 'Hollywoodland'.

- *Star Wars* character Yoda was originally called The Critter.

- John Wayne made an album entitled *America, Why I Love Her*.

- In *Superman*, when Superman discovers Lois Lane's body he lets out a scream, revealing his tooth fillings. Not very in keeping with his invincible image.

- Tom Selleck was originally cast as Indiana Jones.

—— ARTS AND ENTERTAINMENT ——

- Meryl Streep, Dustin Hoffman, Gene Hackman and Burt Lancaster all started out as waiting staff.

- Bruce Willis recently played with his band at the opening of a branch of Krispy Kreme Doughnuts.

- Goldie Hawn and Kurt Russell had a car stolen from their drive and didn't notice for three days.

- Sergeant Bilko's first name is Ernest.

- Paramount is the only major studio still based in Hollywood.

- After breaking up with his fiancée Winona Ryder, Johnny Depp had his tattoo 'Winona Forever' changed to 'Wino Forever'.

- Mickey Rooney's real name is Joe Yule Jnr.

- Bix Beiderbecke was the first white jazz musician.

- George Harrison was president of the George Formby Appreciation Society.

- The difference between animated chipmunks Chip 'n' Dale is that Chip has one tooth and Dale has two.

——— ARTS AND ENTERTAINMENT ———

● Billie Holiday was known as 'Lady Day'.

● There are five basic foot positions in ballet.

● Thirteen or more players are needed for a big band.

● The heavy metal band Black Sabbath got their name from a 1963 horror film of the same name, starring Boris Karloff.

● Johann Strauss was seven years old when he wrote his first waltz.

● Super-heroine Wonder Woman's real name is Diana Prince.

● Verdi's opera *Aida* was commissioned to celebrate the opening of the Suez Canal in 1869.

● Popeye lives on the Island of Sweetwater.

● The Fine Young Cannibals won Best British Group at the 1990 Brit Awards. But the band members returned their trophies, saying that the awards show was being used to promote Margaret Thatcher.

● Prince's nickname is 'His Royal Badness'.

ARTS AND ENTERTAINMENT

- Johnny Cash recorded an album live in Folsom State Prison, in California.

- The TV series *Battlestar Galactica* was the subject of lawsuits from 20th Century Fox, as the company alleged it was a 'steal' from *Star Wars*.

- The cartoon strip 'Peanuts' has appeared in some 2,600 newspapers in 75 countries, and has been translated into 21 languages.

- Chopin made his debut as a pianist at the age of eight.

- Billy Batson must say the name of the ancient wizard 'Shazam' to transform into Captain Marvel.

- Dolly Parton owns a theme park called Dollywood in the Great Smoky Mountains, Tennessee.

- The melody of 'Twinkle, Twinkle Little Star' was composed by Mozart.

- The real name of Batman villain The Penguin is Oswald Chesterfield Cobblepot.

- A total of 364 gifts are given by the lover in 'The Twelve Days of Christmas' song.

——— ARTS AND ENTERTAINMENT ———

- Sting's real name is Gordon Sumner.

- Contralto is the lowest female singing voice.

- Engelbert Humperdinck's real name is Arnold Dorsey.

- Hank Williams was known as the 'Drifting Cowboy'.

- Kazatsky is a Russian folk dance characterised by a step in which a squatting dancer kicks out each leg alternately to the front.

- The taboo against whistling backstage comes from the pre-electricity era, when a whistle was the signal for the curtains and the scenery to drop. An unexpected whistle could cause an unexpected scene change.

- 'The Star-Spangled Banner' is ranked the most difficult national anthem to sing.

- The Writers' Guild of America Registration Office states that approximately 20,000 movie scripts are registered with the Guild each year and that, of these, less than one per cent are picked up by a studio and made into a film.

- The names of the six Gummi bears are Gruffi, Cubbi, Tummi, Zummi, Sunni and Grammi.

——— ARTS AND ENTERTAINMENT ———

- Whistler's best-known painting, often called *Whistler's Mother*, is actually titled *Arrangement in Grey and Black: The Artist's Mother*.

- The names of Popeye's four nephews are Pipeye, Peepeye, Pupeye and Poopeye.

- The Pac Man video arcade game featured coloured ghosts named Inky, Blinky, Pinky and Clyde.

- The Marlboro Man has appeared in more advertisements than any ad figure in history.

- There are 20,000 television commercials made each year that are aimed exclusively at children in the US, with 7,000 for sugared breakfast cereals.

- Ancient Chinese artists freely painted scenes of nakedness but would never depict a bare female foot.

- Nearly 80% of Japanese adverts use celebrities, the majority being local stars. Of the foreign celebrities, the most popular are Arnold Schwarzenegger, promoting noodles, and Steven Spielberg, endorsing whisky.

- The average American sees or hears 560 advertisements a day.

——— ARTS AND ENTERTAINMENT ———

- War photographer Robert Capa's famous photos of D-Day were selected from only 11 exposures that survived the developing process. Although he had shot four rolls of film, most of the photos were ruined by heat.

- In Leonardo da Vinci's famous painting *The Last Supper*, a salt cellar near Judas Iscariot is knocked over. This is said to have started the superstition that spilt salt is unlucky.

- The oldest piano still in existence was built in 1720.

- The average medium-sized piano has about 230 strings, each string having about 165 lb (75 kg) of tension, with the combined pull of all strings equalling approximately 18 tons (18,288 kg).

- X-rays of Leonardo da Vinci's *Mona Lisa* reveal there to be three completely different versions of the same subject, all painted by da Vinci, under the final portrait.

- The sculpture by Auguste Rodin that has come to be called *The Thinker* was not meant to be a profile of a man in thought, but a representation of the poet Dante.

- Because of the precautions taken to prevent photographers from showing the public what occurred on the floor of the New York Stock Exchange, the first

——— **ARTS AND ENTERTAINMENT** ———

published picture, in 1907, was made through an empty coat sleeve that concealed a camera.

- The harp's ancestor is a hunting bow.

- Violins weigh less than 16 oz (approximately 448 g) yet resist string tension of over 65 lb (29 kg).

2

USELESS THINGS PEOPLE SAY

—— USELESS THINGS PEOPLE SAY ——

● 'It's a bit like going to heaven without having to die first.'
Labour MP Tony Banks, on being made Minister for Sport

● 'I'm the master of low expectations.'
US President George W Bush

● 'If your lifeguard duties were as good as your singing, a lot of people would be drowning.'
Simon Cowell, judge on reality TV talent show Pop Idol

● 'I can still enjoy sex at 74 – I live at 75 so it's no distance.'
Comic Bob Monkhouse

● 'The midfield is numerically outnumbered.'
Football pundit Ron Atkinson

● 'Last week I stated that this woman was the ugliest woman I had ever seen. I have since been visited by her sister and now wish to withdraw that statement.'
American writer Mark Twain

● 'Actually, it only takes one drink to get me loaded. Trouble is, I can't remember if it's the thirteenth or fourteenth.'
US comic actor George Burns

USELESS THINGS PEOPLE SAY

- 'Common-looking people are the best in the world: that is the reason the Lord makes so many of them.'
  US President Abraham Lincoln

- 'I bought a dog the other day... I named him Stay. It's fun to call him... "Come here, Stay! Come here, Stay!" He went insane. Now he just ignores me.'
  US comic Stephen Wright

- 'The first thing that ran across my mind was to bite him back'.
  Boxer Evander Holyfield, after rival Mike Tyson bit his ear off during a fight

- 'Women are like elephants. I like to watch them, but I wouldn't want to own one.'
  US actor and writer W C Fields

- 'I like to have a martini, two at the very most. After three I'm under the table. After four I'm under my host.'
  Dorothy Parker, US critic, satirical poet and short-story writer

- 'I myself have never been able to find out precisely what feminism is; I only know that people call me a feminist whenever I express sentiments that differentiate me from a doormat or a prostitute.'
  Irish writer Rebecca West

———— USELESS THINGS PEOPLE SAY ————

- 'If you want to see a comic strip, you should see me in the shower.'
  US comic actor Groucho Marx

- 'A verbal contract isn't worth the paper it's written on.'
  Hollywood film producer Sam Goldwyn

- 'To find out a girl's faults, praise her to her girlfriends.'
  US statesman and inventor Benjamin Franklin

- 'Coping with the language shouldn't be a problem. I can't speak English.'
  Footballer Paul Gascoigne, on moving to Italian club Lazio

- 'A pun is the lowest form of humour — when you don't think of it first.'
  US pianist and actor Oscar Levant

- 'I want a sandwich named after me.'
  US comic Jon Stewart

- 'I love New York City; I've got a gun.'
  Basketball player Charles Barkley

- 'No one knows my ability the way I do. I am pushing against it all the time.'
  US author John Steinbeck

USELESS THINGS PEOPLE SAY

- 'It's just a job. Grass grows, birds fly, waves pound the sand. I beat people up.'
  Heavyweight champion Muhammad Ali

- 'I'm not smart enough to lie.'
  US President Ronald Reagan

- 'Hollywood is a place where they'll pay you 50,000 dollars for a kiss and 50 cents for your soul.'
  Hollywood movie star Marilyn Monroe

- 'Being a celebrity is probably the closest to being a beautiful woman as you can get.'
  US actor Kevin Costner

- 'You have to be a bastard to make it, and that's a fact. And the Beatles are the biggest bastards on earth.'
  John Lennon, musician, writer, actor and activist

- 'You can see our respect for women by the fact that we have pledged to pay working women, even though they don't have to work.'
  Taliban Information Minister Amir Khan Muttaqi

- 'If I die before my cat, I want a little of my ashes put in his food so I can live inside him.'
  US actress Drew Barrymore

———— USELESS THINGS PEOPLE SAY ————

- 'If you're going through hell, keep going.'
  US animator and film producer Walt Disney

- 'Every man wishes to be wise, and they who cannot be wise are almost always cunning.'
  US actor Samuel L Jackson

- 'I want a man who's kind and understanding. Is that too much to ask of a millionaire?'
  Hollywood actress Zsa Zsa Gabor

- 'The streets are safe in Philadelphia. It's only the people who make them unsafe.'
  Frank Rizzo, ex-police chief and mayor of Philadelphia

- 'People used to throw rocks at me because of my clothes. Now they wanna know where I buy them.'
  Singer Cyndi Lauper

- 'During the scrimmage, Tarkanian paced the sideline with his hands in his pockets while biting his nails.'
  Report describing basketball coach Jerry Tarkanian

- 'Maybe there is no actual place called hell. Maybe hell is just having to listen to our grandparents breathe through their noses when they're eating sandwiches.'
  Actor Jim Carrey

USELESS THINGS PEOPLE SAY

- 'A billion here, a billion there, sooner or later it adds up to real money.'
  Congressman Everett Dirksen

- 'If I hadn't been a woman, I'd have been a drag queen.'
  Country singer Dolly Parton

- 'I get to go to lots of overseas places, like Canada.'
  Singer Britney Spears

- 'Middle age is when your age starts to show around your middle.'
  US comedian and actor Bob Hope

- 'I've been on a calendar, but I've never been on time.'
  Marilyn Monroe

- 'The only place where success comes before work is in a dictionary.'
  Entrepreneur Vidal Sassoon

- 'Time you enjoy wasting, was not wasted.'
  John Lennon

- 'If you would be singing like this two thousand years ago, people would have stoned you.'
  Simon Cowell, speaking on Pop Idol

——— USELESS THINGS PEOPLE SAY ———

- 'Our nation must come together to unite.'
  George W Bush

- 'I'm not saying my wife's a bad cook, but she uses a smoke alarm as a timer.'
  Comic Bob Monkhouse

- 'For me their biggest threat is when they get into the attacking part of the field.'
  Football pundit Ron Atkinson

- 'Sex is better than talk. Talk is what you suffer through so you can get to sex.'
  Woody Allen, US actor, director and comedian

- 'Give me a museum and I'll fill it.'
  Spanish Cubist painter and sculptor Pablo Picasso

- 'Military intelligence is a contradiction in terms.'
  Groucho Marx
- 'Giving up smoking is easy... I've done it hundreds of times.'
  Mark Twain

- 'Every time I look at you I get a fierce desire to be lonesome.'
  Oscar Levant

──── USELESS THINGS PEOPLE SAY ────

- 'Ever notice how it's a penny for your thoughts, yet you put in your two cents? Someone is making a penny on the deal!'
  US comic Stephen Wright

- 'If you steal from one author, it's plagiarism; if you steal from many, it's research.'
  US screenwriter Wilson Mizner

- 'The laziest man I ever met put popcorn in his pancakes so they would turn over by themselves.'
  W C Fields

- 'There are three faithful friends: an old wife, an old dog, and ready money.'
  Benjamin Franklin

- 'Hull is very nice. The weather is very like home.'
  Hull City's Spanish footballer Antonio Doncel-Valcarcel

- 'If people screw me, I screw back in spades.'
  US billionaire Donald Trump

- 'I wasn't the cutest or the most talented, but I could get through the question–and–answer period.'
  Talk-show presenter Oprah Winfrey, commenting on beauty pageants

———— USELESS THINGS PEOPLE SAY ————

- 'Charlie Brown is the one person I identify with. CB is such a loser. He wasn't even the star of his own Halloween special.'
  US comic Chris Rock

- 'I never set out to hurt anybody deliberately unless it was, you know, important. Like a league game or something.'
  American footballer Dick Butkus

- 'I dress for women, and undress for men.'
  US actress Angie Dickinson

- 'The problem with people who have no vices is that generally you can be pretty sure they're going to have some pretty annoying virtues.'
  British actress Elizabeth Taylor

- 'If you suck on a tit, the movie gets an R rating. If you hack the tit off with an axe, it will be PG.'
  US actor Jack Nicholson

- 'I feel safe in white because, deep down inside, I'm an angel.'
  Rapper and producer P-Diddy

- 'One man with courage is a majority.'
  US President Thomas Jefferson

--------- **USELESS THINGS PEOPLE SAY** ---------

- 'I was like, "I want that one!" '
  US pop princess Jessica Simpson, speaking about boyfriend Nick Lachey of boyband 98 Degrees

- 'By the time you're 80 years old you've learned everything. You only have to remember it.'
  George Burns

- 'Being married means I can break wind and eat ice-cream in bed.'
  US actor Brad Pitt

- 'How many husbands have I had? You mean apart from my own?'
  Zsa Zsa Gabor

- 'It's so sweet, I feel like my teeth are rotting when I listen to the radio.'
  Irish singer and activist Bono

- 'I think the team that wins Game 5 will win the series. Unless we lose Game 5.'
  Charles Barkley

- 'You're not drunk if you can lie on the floor without holding on.'
  US actor and singer Dean Martin

———— USELESS THINGS PEOPLE SAY ————

● 'We're going to move left and right at the same time.'
Jerry Brown, Governor of California

● 'TV has brought murder back into the home where it belongs.'
Master film director Alfred Hitchcock

● 'When you are down and out, something always turns up – usually the noses of your friends.'
US actor, writer and director Orson Welles

● 'Wise men talk because they have something to say. Fools talk because they have to say something.'
Greek philosopher Plato

● 'Football players win football games.'
Chuck Knox, American football coach

● 'Traditionally, most of Australia's imports come from overseas.'
Former Australian cabinet minister Keppel Enderbery

● 'I wanted to perform, I wanted to write songs, and I wanted to get lots of chicks.'
Musician James Taylor, when asked why he got into music

● 'Beer is proof that God loves us and wants us to be happy.'
Benjamin Franklin

———— USELESS THINGS PEOPLE SAY ————

- 'I'm not against half-naked girls – not as often as I'd like to be...'
  British comedian Benny Hill

- 'Ever wonder if illiterate people get the full effect of alphabet soup?'
  US comic John Mendoza

- 'Love is the only force capable of transforming an enemy into a friend.'
  US civil-rights leader Martin Luther King Jnr

- 'After *The Wizard of Oz* I was typecast as a lion, and there aren't all that many parts for lions.'
  Actor Bert Lahr

- 'I've had a wonderful evening, but this wasn't it.'
  Groucho Marx

- 'I can answer you in two words – im possible.'
  Sam Goldwyn

- 'Don't stay in bed, unless you can make money in bed.'
  George Burns

- 'Denial ain't just a river in Egypt.'
  Mark Twain

———— USELESS THINGS PEOPLE SAY ————

- 'Sport is like the theatre. People want to see good-looking people who are dressed properly.'
  Tennis star Anna Kournikova

- 'Real happiness is when you marry a girl for love and find out later she has money.'
  Bob Monkhouse

- 'If the Cameroons get a goal back here, they're literally gonna catch on fire.'
  Ron Atkinson

- 'I was thrown out of college for cheating on the metaphysics exam: I looked into the soul of another boy.'
  Woody Allen

- 'I like pigs. Dogs look up to us. Cats look down on us. Pigs treat us as equals.'
  British Prime Minister Winston Churchill

- 'Who is General Failure, and why is he reading my hard disk?'
  US comic Stephen Wright

- 'I never forget a face, but in your case I'll make an exception.'
  Groucho Marx

——— USELESS THINGS PEOPLE SAY ———

- 'I am free of all prejudices. I hate everyone equally.'
  W C Fields

- 'They misunderestimated me.'
  George W Bush

- 'Anybody that walks can sing.'
  Michael Stipe, REM singer

- 'I once said cynically of a politician, "He'll double-cross that bridge when he comes to it." '
  Oscar Levant

- 'It's better to live one day as a lion, than a hundred as a sheep.'
  Italian Fascist statesman and Prime Minister Benito Mussolini

- 'Everything I buy is vintage and smells funny. Maybe that's why I don't have a boyfriend.'
  Actress Lucy Liu

- 'I don't listen to music. I hate all music.'
  Johnny Rotten, Sex Pistols vocalist

- 'Because young men are so goddamn disappointing!'
  US actor Harrison Ford, commenting on why women like older leading men

—— USELESS THINGS PEOPLE SAY ——

- 'Everybody stands – that's our policy. If Jesus Christ comes on the show, guess what? It's like, "Stand right here, Jesus, we got Papa Roach coming up at number six." '
  MTV host Carson Daly

- 'I think that the film *Clueless* was very deep. I think it was deep in the way that it was very light. I think lightness has to come from a very deep place if it's true lightness.'
  US actress Alicia Silverstone

- 'Cocaine is God's way of saying you're making too much money.'
  US actor and comedian Robin Williams

- 'I've always wanted to be a spy, and frankly I'm a little surprised that British intelligence has never approached me.'
  Actress and model Elizabeth Hurley

- 'Women are meant to be loved, not to be understood.'
  Oscar Wilde, Irish dramatist, novelist, poet and wit

- 'The only reason we're 7–0 is because we've won all seven of our games.'
  David Garcia, baseball team manager

——— USELESS THINGS PEOPLE SAY ———

- 'It's about the two Ms – movement and positioning.'
  Ron Atkinson

- 'Run for office? No. I've slept with too many women,
  I've done too many drugs, and I've been to too many
  parties.'
  US actor George Clooney

- 'With all due respect to the world's great drummers – it
  ain't brain surgery.'
  Mickey Dolenz, The Monkees singer and drummer

- 'It is full of interest. It has noble poetry in it; and some
  clever fables; and some blood-drenched history; and
  some good morals; and a wealth of obscenity; and
  upwards of a thousand lies.'
  Mark Twain, commenting on the Bible

- 'TV is more interesting than people. If it were not, we
  should have people standing in the corners of our
  rooms.'
  British satirist Alan Coren

- 'Chemistry is a class you take in high school or college,
  where you figure out two plus two is 10, or something.'
  *Basketball player Dennis Rodman, speaking about Chicago
  Bull's team chemistry being overrated*

—— USELESS THINGS PEOPLE SAY ——

- 'Golf is a game whose aim is to hit a very small ball into an even smaller hole, with weapons singularly ill-designed for the purpose.'
  Winston Churchill

- 'I am an optimist. But I'm an optimist who takes his raincoat.'
  British Prime Minister Harold Wilson

- 'I'm an excellent housekeeper. Every time I get a divorce, I keep the house.'
  Zsa Zsa Gabor

- 'A hippie is someone who looks like Tarzan, walks like Jane and smells like Cheetah.'
  Ronald Reagan

- 'I cannot sing, dance or act; what else would I be but a talk-show host.'
  US talk-show host David Letterman

- 'What's another word for thesaurus?'
  Steven Wright

- 'Keep your eyes wide open before marriage, and half-shut afterwards.'
  Benjamin Franklin

——— USELESS THINGS PEOPLE SAY ———

- 'We spent a lot of time talking about Africa, as we should. Africa is a nation that suffers from incredible disease.'
  George W Bush

- 'When the inventor of the drawing board messed things up ... what did he go back to?'
  Bob Monkhouse

- 'I'm living on a one-way, dead-end street. I don't know how I got there.'
  Stephen Wright

- ''Twas a woman who drove me to drink. I never had the courtesy to thank her.'
  W C Fields

- 'I'd love to be a pop idol. Of course, my groupies are now between 40 and 50.'
  Actor Kevin Bacon

- 'There's nothing sexier than a lapsed Catholic.'
  Woody Allen

- 'I've given up reading books. I find it takes my mind off myself.'
  Oscar Levant

———— USELESS THINGS PEOPLE SAY ————

● 'Gentlemen – include me out.'
  Sam Goldwyn

● 'A bit of lusting after someone does wonders for the skin.'
  Elizabeth Hurley

● 'What does this Frenchman know about football? He
  wears glasses and looks like a schoolteacher. Does he
  even speak English properly?'
  *Arsenal captain Tony Adams, speaking about new boss Arsene
  Wenger*

● 'Those are my principles. If you don't like them, I have
  others.'
  Groucho Marx

● 'Retire? I'm going to stay in show business until I'm the
  only one left.'
  George Burns at age 90

● 'Feminism is just a way for ugly women to get into the
  mainstream of America.'
  Right-wing talk-show host Rush Limbaugh

● 'Security is the essential road-block to achieving the
  road-map to peace.'
  George W Bush

—————— **USELESS THINGS PEOPLE SAY** ——————

- 'I do my best work when I'm in pain and turmoil.'
  Sting

- 'The largest crowd ever in the state of Las Vegas.'
  Mark Jones, TV Broadcaster

- 'It's funny the way most people love the dead. Once you are dead, you are made for life.'
  Genius guitar player Jimi Hendrix

- 'Coming on to pitch is Mike Moore, who is six foot one and 212 years old.'
  Sportscaster Herb Score

- 'Those who dance are considered insane by those who cannot hear the music.'
  Comic George Carlin

- 'I could take Sean Connery in a fight... I could definitely take him.'
  Harrison Ford

- 'Man – a figment of God's imagination.'
  Mark Twain

- 'I'm a 4-wheel-drive pickup type of guy. So is my wife.'
  Baseball player Mike Greenwell

—— USELESS THINGS PEOPLE SAY ——

● 'We don't want the television script good. We want it Tuesday.'
TV writer Dennis Norden

● 'We didn't think about its proper use. We just wanted something to be weird, and the umlaut is very visual. It's German and strong, and that Nazi Germany mentality – "the future belongs to us" – intrigued me.'
US rocker Nikki Sixx, explaining the use of umlauts over the 'o' and 'u' of 'Mötley Crüe'

● 'I know what I believe. I will continue to articulate what I believe and what I believe – I believe what I believe is right.'
George W Bush

● 'What's a geriatric? A German footballer scoring three goals.'
Bob Monkhouse

● 'History will be kind to me for I intend to write it.'
Winston Churchill

● 'Good enough for the homeless but not for an international striker.'
Footballer Pierre Van Hooijdonk, on his rejection of a £7,000-a-week pay increase offer at Celtic

——— USELESS THINGS PEOPLE SAY ———

● 'An eye for an eye makes the whole world blind.'
Gandhi, Indian nationalist and spiritual leader

● 'Some are born great, some achieve greatness, and some hire PR officers.'
Pulitzer Prize-winning author Daniel J Boorstin

● 'God heals and the doctor takes the fee.'
Benjamin Franklin

● 'There are worst things than death. If you've ever spent an evening with an insurance salesman, you know exactly what I mean.'
Woody Allen

● 'The keeper was unsighted – he still didn't see it.'
Ron Atkinson

● 'All those who believe in telekinesis, raise my hand.'
Stephen Wright

● 'I've been accused of vulgarity. I say that's bullshit.'
US actor and comedian Mel Brooks

● 'Once I shot an elephant in my pyjamas. How he got into my pyjamas, I'll never know.'
Groucho Marx

USELESS THINGS PEOPLE SAY

● 'My audience loves to see Britney get her head cut off.'
Rocker Alice Cooper

● 'You've also got to measure in order to begin to effect change that's just more – when there's more than talk, there's just actual – a paradigm shift.'
George W Bush

● 'Let's bring it up to date with some snappy 19th-century dialogue.'
Sam Goldwyn

● 'Roses are red, violets are blue, I'm schizophrenic, and so am I.'
Oscar Levant

● 'All of the Mets' road wins against Los Angeles this year have been at Dodger Stadium.'
Sportscaster Ralph Kiner

● 'When I am dead, I hope it may be said: "His sins were scarlet but his books were read."'
Writer Hilaire Belloc

● 'Shoot a few scenes out of focus. I want to win the foreign film award.'
Film-maker Billy Wilder

——— USELESS THINGS PEOPLE SAY ———

- 'Television: A medium. So called because it's neither rare nor well done.'
  US comic Ernie Kovacs

- 'You're not a real manager unless you've been sacked.'
  Football manager Malcolm Allison

- 'I wish to be cremated. One-tenth of my ashes shall be given to my agent, as written in our contract.'
  Groucho Marx

- 'I hate to advocate drugs, alcohol, violence, or insanity to anyone, but they've always worked for me.'
  Author Hunter S Thompson

- 'I wanted a name that would put us first in the phone directory, or second if you count ABBA...'
  ABC singer Martin Fry

- 'Build a man a fire, and he'll be warm for a day. Set a man on fire, and he'll be warm for the rest of his life.'
  British author Terry Pratchett

- 'In Russia we only had two TV channels. Channel One was propaganda. Channel Two consisted of a KGB officer telling you: Turn back at once to Channel One.'
  Russian comic Yakov Smirnoff

———— USELESS THINGS PEOPLE SAY ————

- 'People think we make $3 million and $4 million a year.
  They don't realise that most of us only make $500,000.'
  Baseball player Pete Incaviglia

- 'You miss 100 per cent of the shots you never take.'
  Hockey player Wayne Gretzky

- 'After two days in hospital I took a turn for the nurse.'
  W C Fields

- 'The length of a film should be directly related to the
  endurance of the human bladder.'
  Alfred Hitchcock

- 'I grew up with six brothers. That's how I learned to
  dance – waiting for the bathroom.'
  Bob Hope

- 'Thanks, you don't look so hot yourself.'
  Baseball player Yogi Berra, after being told he looked cool

- 'The last time I was inside a woman was when I was
  inside the Statue of Liberty.'
  Woody Allen

- 'In Australia, not reading poetry is the national pastime.'
  US poet Phyllis McGinley

─────── **USELESS THINGS PEOPLE SAY** ───────

● 'I think the American people – I hope the American –
I don't think, let me – I hope the American people
trust me.'
George W Bush

● 'Never hold discussions with the monkey when the
organ grinder is in the room.'
Winston Churchill

● 'The light at the end of the tunnel has been turned off
due to budget cuts.'
US comic Stephen Wright

● 'We're going to turn this team around 360 degrees.'
Basketball player Jason Kidd

● 'What we want is a story that starts with an earthquake
and works its way up to a climax.'
Producer Sam Goldwyn

● 'Guests, like fish, begin to smell after three days.'
Benjamin Franklin

● 'You can tell German wine from vinegar by the label.'
Mark Twain

● 'Christmas at my house is always at least six or seven

—————— USELESS THINGS PEOPLE SAY ——————

times more pleasant than anywhere else. We start
drinking early. And while everyone else is seeing only
one Santa Claus, we'll be seeing six or seven.'
W C Fields

● 'I resign. I wouldn't want to belong to any club that
would have me as a member.'
Groucho Marx

● 'On another night, they'd have won 2–2.'
Football pundit Ron Atkinson

● 'I agree the lad's pace can be deceptive. He's much
slower than you think.'
Liverpool manager Bill Shankly on footballer Roy Evans

● 'So little time and so little to do.'
US pianist and actor Oscar Levant

● 'They say such nice things about people at their funerals
that it makes me sad that I'm going to miss mine by just
a few days.'
Writer Garrison Keilor

● 'Beware of the man who denounces women writers; his
penis is tiny and he cannot spell.'
US writer and feminist Erica Jong

———— USELESS THINGS PEOPLE SAY ————

● 'Life's tragedy is that we get old too soon and wise too late.'
Benjamin Franklin

● 'When did I realise I was God? Well, I was praying and I suddenly realised I was talking to myself.'
British actor Peter O'Toole

● 'This is not a novel to be tossed aside lightly. It should be thrown with great force.'
Dorothy Parker

● 'In Hollywood, if you don't have happiness you send out for it.'
Actor Rex Reed

● 'An author who speaks about their own books is almost as bad as a mother who speaks about her own children.'
Benjamin Disraeli, British Tory statesman and Prime Minister

● 'I don't bring God into my life to … to, you know, kind of be a political person.'
George W Bush

● 'A man's got to believe in something. I believe I'll have another drink.'
W C Fields

———— USELESS THINGS PEOPLE SAY ————

- 'Of all the things I've lost, I miss my mind the most.'
  Mark Twain

- 'Zero–zero is a big score.'
  Ron Atkinson

- 'There's a fine line between genius and insanity. I have erased this line.'
  Oscar Levant

- 'This film cost $31 million. With that kind of money I could have invaded some country.'
  US actor and director Clint Eastwood

- 'Immature poets imitate; mature poets steal.'
  T S Eliot, American-born British poet, critic and dramatist

- 'It's amazing I won. I was running against peace, prosperity and incumbency.'
  George W Bush, speaking to the Swedish Prime Minister and unaware that a live television camera was still rolling

- 'I was married by a judge. I should have asked for a jury.'
  Groucho Marx

- 'Wise men don't need advice. Fools won't take it.'
  Benjamin Franklin

———— USELESS THINGS PEOPLE SAY ————

- 'It took me 15 years to discover that I had no talent for writing, but I couldn't give it up because by that time I was too famous.'
  US actor, author and humorist Robert Benchley

- 'There's only one person who hugs the mothers and the widows, the wives and the kids upon the death of their loved one. Others hug but having committed the troops, I've got an additional responsibility to hug and that's me and I know what it's like.'
  George W Bush

- 'You know when you put a stick in water and it looks bent? That's why I never take baths.'
  US comic Stephen Wright

- 'Ah, the patter of little feet around the house. There's nothing like having a midget for a butler.'
  W C Fields

- 'What the world needs is more geniuses with humility, there are so few of us left.'
  US pianist and actor Oscar Levant

- 'I don't want any yes-men around me. I want everyone to tell me the truth – even if it costs him his job.'
  Producer Samuel Goldwyn

———— USELESS THINGS PEOPLE SAY ————

● 'We've all passed a lot of water since then.'
Producer Sam Goldwyn

● 'Outside a dog, a book is a man's best friend. Inside a dog, it's too dark to read.'
Groucho Marx

● 'There are two sides to every question: my side and the wrong side.'
US pianist and actor Oscar Levant

● 'The only imaginative fiction being written today is income tax returns.'
Pulitzer Prize-winning author Herman Wouk

● 'You're free. And freedom is beautiful. And, you know, it'll take time to restore chaos and order – order out of chaos. But we will.'
George W Bush

● 'Someone told me that each equation I included in the book would halve the sales.'
Stephen Hawking, about A Brief History of Time

● 'My answer is bring them on.'
George W Bush, commenting on Iraqi militants attacking US forces

———— USELESS THINGS PEOPLE SAY ————

- 'Underneath this flabby exterior is an enormous lack of character.'
  US pianist and actor Oscar Levant
  George W Bush.

- 'I trust the people.'
  George W Bush before the election

- 'People can't be trusted.'
  Bush after the election

- 'Critics are to authors what dogs are to lamp-posts.'
  US author Jeffrey Robinson

- 'How did I get to Hollywood? By train.'
  Film-maker John Ford

- 'Buy land. They've stopped making it.'
  Mark Twain

3

ELVIS

———————————— ELVIS ————————————

- Elvis's first girlfriend was childhood sweetheart 16-year-old Dixie Locke, a high-school senior who was his first prom date.

- Elvis was born at 4.36 a.m. on 8 January 1935 at the home of his parents, Gladys and Vernon Presley, in Old Bailey Road, East Tupelo, Mississippi.

- He weighed 5 lb (2 kg) at birth and was the second of twins. His older brother, Jesse Aaron, was stillborn at 4 a.m.

- In October 1945, at age 10, Elvis won second prize in a talent contest, singing the tearjerker 'Old Shep' at the Mississippi-Alabama Fair and Dairy Show in Tupelo.

- Elvis's mother bought him his first guitar, costing $7.75, at a Tupelo hardware store as a present for his 11th birthday.

- At his first public appearance, with the L C Humes High School band in April 1963, his name was misspelled 'Elvis Prestly' on the programme.

- On his first billed appearance, at the Overton Park Shell, Memphis, in the summer of 1964, a newspaper advertisement referred to him as 'Ellis Presley'.

ELVIS

- When Elvis's first record was released he was a semi-illiterate truck driver.

- His first commercial recording session took place in the Sun Records studio in Memphis on 5 July 1954. He taped 'Harbour Lights', and after a break, recorded 'That's All Right (Mama)' and 'Blue Moon of Kentucky' with Scotty Moore and Bill Black.

- Scotty Moore and disc jockey Bob Neal were Elvis's managers before he signed with self-styled 'Colonel' Tom Parker, a former dog catcher and carnival barker, on 15 March 1956.

- Parker, an illegal immigrant from the Netherlands in 1929, who claimed to have been born in Virginia, went on to shamefully mishandle Elvis's career – taking a 50% cut on all Elvis's earnings, as well as lucrative fees for granting contracts. He made more money than his client.

- After his conscription in the army, mainly served in Germany, Elvis returned to the United States on 5 March 1960, and was honourably discharged at Fort Dix.

- Since his death Elvis is said to have been spotted by scores of witnesses both in the United States and other countries.

ELVIS

- Elvis recorded more than 650 songs – 18 of his singles reaching number one in the charts. With a three-octave voice, his number-one hits covered a range of styles, including country, gospel, rock 'n' roll, rhythm and blues, and pop.

- In 1957, at age 22, Elvis bought Graceland. It was a 23-room mansion 10 miles (16 km) south of Memphis, which, with various outbuildings, stood in 13.8 acres of land. It overlooked Route 51, which was later renamed Elvis Presley Boulevard. He paid $100,000 cash for the property.

- Major Bill Smith, a record producer who met Elvis in 1956, says he talked to Elvis after his supposed death and received two remarkable cassettes in the mail, allegedly sent by the King. A police voice identification expert from Houston compared one of the tapes with an Elvis interview from 1962 and found a staggering 35 instances where the voice patterns matched.

- The biggest Elvis hit, 'Heartbreak Hotel', was written in just 22 minutes by retired dishwasher repairman Tommy Durden and Nashville songwriter Mae Boren Axton.

- Elvis's longest-running single in the Top 100 chart was 'All Shook Up', which lasted an incredible 30 weeks – with eight straight weeks at number one.

―――――――――― **ELVIS** ――――――――――

- Elvis produced a staggering 45 gold records, each one selling over a million copies. No artist had ever been credited with such staggering record sales, until Elvis proved it could be done.

- Gail Brewer Giorgio, author of *Is Elvis Alive?*, released an hour-long cassette of an alleged conversation with Elvis, recorded four years after his death. Elvis talks of travelling around Europe, his need for privacy and his wish to resume his career – all in the familiar, low, slightly slurred drawl.

- Elvis and Priscilla divorced on 11 October 1973. He had several girlfriends afterwards. The last was Ginger Aiden, who found him sprawled on the bathroom floor at 2.30 p.m. on 18 August 1977. She said they had planned to marry on Christmas Day. Elvis had already ordered a £27,600 ring.

- Partly because of his wild spending, and partly because 'Colonel' Parker took such a huge slice of his income, Elvis had only £2.75 million when he died. His estate has made more since his death than he made when he was alive.

- For Elvis, *Loving You* was a family affair, as both his mother and father appeared on camera in the production.

ELVIS

- Elvis's first screen kiss came in his second movie, *Loving You*, when actress Jana Lund made screen history by being the first woman to kiss Elvis on film. It was also his first colour movie.

- Elvis was touchy about his height and secretly wore lifts in his shoes to make him appear taller.

- Elvis's favourite actress was Shelley Fabares, who appeared in three of his films.

- If he wanted to book seats or travel incognito, Elvis frequently used the names Dr John Carpenter or John Burrows Jnr.

- Elvis was a big animal-lover and his many pets at Graceland included cats, dogs, ducks, fish, ponies, peacocks, a parrot and a chimpanzee.

- Priscilla Ann Beaulieu was just 14, a grey-eyed, 5 ft 3 (1.5 m) schoolgirl, when Elvis fell in love with her while serving in the army in Germany. Her stepfather was a US Air Force Captain.

- The first music Elvis Aaron Presley ever heard was in his early years at the First Assembly of God Church, in East Tupelo, Mississippi.

ELVIS

- *Love Me Tender* was Elvis's first movie. He played opposite veteran stars Debra Paget and Richard Egan.

- Elvis proposed to Priscilla on Christmas Eve 1966. They married at the Aladdin Hotel in Las Vegas on 1 May 1967. The wedding ring had a three-carat diamond surrounded by 20 other diamonds.

- In 1948, when Elvis was 13, the family packed its belongings in cardboard boxes and paper bags, and moved to Memphis in their 1939 Packard.

- On 14 August 1958 Gladys Presley died of a heart attack, brought on by acute hepatitis, at the Methodist Hospital in Memphis. Elvis was devastated.

- Exactly nine months after the wedding, on 1 February 1968, Lisa Marie Presley was born in Memphis. Had she been a boy, they would have named him John Baron Presley.

- Elvis made 31 movies but desperately wanted more substantial, challenging roles. However, 'Colonel' Parker and the movie moguls saw a source of easy money in his mindless, low-budget films. They used the huge profits to bankroll more important movies, featuring established big stars.

4

ROYALS

ROYALS

- Greenwich Palace was Henry VIII's favourite residence.

- Henry VIII was probably the most athletic monarch, enjoying tennis, archery and wrestling.

- In the 17th century, the Great Hall at Westminster Palace was used as a shopping precinct.

- The first prisoner in the Tower of London, Ranulf Flambard, Bishop of Durham, escaped down a rope smuggled to him in a flagon of wine.

- George III said he didn't like Hampton Court, due to memories of being hit on the ears by his grandfather there as a boy.

- Hot water and clothes were sent to Prince Albert's room every morning after his death. The glass he sipped his last medicine from lay unmoved on the table next to his bed for 40 years.

- Charles II was a keen tennis player and would weigh himself before and after every game to see how much weight he had lost.

- William III and his wife Mary hated Whitehall Palace, as it was bad for William's asthma.

ROYALS

- The Tower of London was once used as a zoo.

- A cannonball, fired in salute, accidentally crashed into Greenwich Palace. It fell into the very room where Mary I was sat, but she was unharmed.

- Extensions to Greenwich Palace conflicted with the main road from Deptford to Woolwich, so it was built on either side, with a bridge joining the two halves until the road was diverted.

- Queen Anne is said to have died from a fit of apoplexy, due to overeating, while at an outdoor supper party at Kensington Palace.

- The drains at Windsor Castle were faulty, allegedly causing the death of Prince Albert.

- A man attempted to assassinate Queen Mary I by climbing atop St James's Palace and using a large lens to focus the sun's rays on her walking below. It failed.

- It was quite common for Westminster Palace to flood with mud and fish from the River Thames, and once rowing boats had to be used in the Great Hall.

- Whitehall Palace once contained a chemical laboratory.

ROYALS

- George II died in his water closet at Kensington Palace, deterring later monarchs from living there.

- Henry III kept a quartet of lions in the Tower of London. They were called Fanny, Miss Fanny, Miss Howe and Miss Fanny Howe.

- James I introduced a swear box to St James's Palace, and all the money was given to the poor.

- King Charles I's dog accompanied him to his execution.

- Queen Anne banned the wearing of spectacles, inappropriate wigs and the smoking of pipes from St James's Palace.

- Queen Victoria referred to Kensington Palace as 'the poor old palace'.

- George II sold tickets to allow the public to watch the King and Queen eat.

- Prince Albert was Queen Victoria's first cousin as well as husband.

- King James VI banned the use of the surname MacGregor.

——— ROYALS ———

- Henry III received a polar bear from the King of Norway. It was allowed to hunt for fish in the River Thames on the end of a long rope.

- At royal banquets, the salt cellar was always the first thing to be laid on the table.

- The first elephant in England was a gift to King Henry III from the King of France.

- William IV considered turning Buckingham Palace into army barracks.

- Charles II had many dogs, and at official meetings of state he preferred playing with them to listening to the discussion.

- Prince Charles and Prince William never travel on the same plane as a precaution against a potential crash.

- The only house in England that the Queen may not enter is the House of Commons, as she is not a commoner.

- When the Duchess of Windsor's jewels were going on the auction block in 1987, Sotheby's sold 24,000 of its pricey catalogues.

ROYALS

- There are 1,783 diamonds on Britain's Imperial State Crown. This includes the 309-carat Star of Africa.

5

INSULTS

INSULTS

- 'He is racist, he's homophobic, he's xenophobic and he's a sexist. He's the perfect Republican candidate.'
  Liberal political commentator Bill Press, speaking about Pat Buchanan

- 'Am reserving two tickets for you for my premiere. Come and bring a friend – if you have one.'
  George Bernard Shaw to Winston Churchill

- 'Impossible to be present for the first performance. Will attend second – if there is one.'
  Winston Churchill, in reply to George Bernard Shaw

- 'You can't see as well as these fucking flowers – and they're fucking plastic.'
  Tennis player John McEnroe, speaking to a line judge

- 'You're like a pay toilet, aren't you? You don't give a shit for nothing.'
  Producer Howard Hughes to actor Robert Mitchum

- 'Who picks your clothes – Stevie Wonder?'
  US comic Don Rickles to talk-show host David Letterman

- 'He has never been known to use a word that might send a reader to the dictionary.'
  William Faulkner, speaking about Ernest Hemingway

INSULTS

- 'If I were married to you, I'd put poison in your coffee.'
  Lady Astor to Winston Churchill

- 'If you were my wife, I'd drink it.'
  Winston Churchill, in reply to Lady Astor

- 'Sir, you're drunk!'
  Lady Astor to Winston Churchill

- 'Yes, madam, I am drunk. But in the morning I will be sober and you will still be ugly.'
  Winston Churchill, replying to Lady Astor

- 'Poor Faulkner. Does he really think big emotions come from big words?'
  Ernest Hemingway's response to William Faulkner

- 'Joe Frazier is so ugly, he should donate his face to the US Bureau of Wildlife.'
  Muhammad Ali's response to Joe Frazier

- 'He got a reputation as a great actor by just thinking hard about the next line.'
  Director King Vidor, speaking about Gary Cooper

- 'He's phoney, using his blackness to get his way.'
  Joe Frazier, speaking about Muhammad Ali

INSULTS

- 'The only reason he had a child is so that he can meet babysitters.'
  US talk-show host David Letterman, speaking about
  Warren Beatty

- 'Do you mind if I sit back a little? Because your breath is very bad.'
  Donald Trump to interviewer Larry King

- 'He's the type of man who will end up dying in his own arms.'
  Actress Mamie Van Doren, speaking about Warren Beatty

- 'He couldn't adlib a fart after a baked-bean dinner.'
  US talk-show host Johnny Carson, speaking about
  Chevy Chase

- 'He acts like he's got a Mixmaster up his ass and doesn't want anyone to know it.'
  Marlon Brando, speaking about Montgomery Clift

- 'His ears made him look like a taxicab with both doors open.'
  Producer Howard Hughes, speaking about Clark Gable

- 'Steve Martin has basically one joke and he's it.'
  Musician Dave Felton

——————— **INSULTS** ———————

- 'Now there sits a man with an open mind. You can feel the draught from here.'
  Groucho Marx, speaking about his brother Chico

- 'Do you mind if I smoke?'
  Oscar Wilde to actress Sarah Bernhardt

- 'I don't care if you burn.'
  Sarah Bernhardt, in reply to Oscar Wilde

- 'Most of the time he sounds like he has a mouth full of wet toilet paper.'
  Actor Rex Reed, speaking about Marlon Brando

- 'I've got three words for him: Am. A. Teur.'
  Former hell-raising actor Charlie Sheen, speaking about current hell-raising actor Colin Farrell

- 'He sings like he's throwing up.'
  Musician Andrew O'Connor, speaking about Bryan Ferry

- 'Well at least he has finally found his true love. What a pity he can't marry himself.'
  Frank Sinatra, speaking about Robert Redford

- 'Bambi with testosterone.'
  Film critic Owen Gleiberman, speaking about Prince

—————————————— **INSULTS** ——————————————

- 'There were three things that Chico was always on – a
  phone, a horse or a broad.'
  Groucho Marx

- 'Arnold Schwarzenegger looks like a condom full of
  walnuts.'
  TV critic and journalist Clive James

- 'McEnroe was as charming as always, which means that
  he was as charming as a dead mouse in a loaf of bread.'
  Clive James

- 'Michael Jackson's album was only called *Bad* because
  there wasn't enough room on the sleeve for 'Pathetic'.
  US songwriter Prince

- 'I love his work but I couldn't warm to him even if I was
  cremated next to him.'
  Keith Richards, speaking about Chuck Berry

- 'Boy George is all England needs – another queen who
  can't dress.'
  US comedienne Joan Rivers

- 'Michael Jackson was a poor black boy who grew up to
  be a rich white woman.'
  Author Molly Ivins

INSULTS

- 'He has turned almost alarmingly blond – he's gone past platinum, he must be plutonium; his hair is co-ordinated with his teeth.'
  Film critic Pauline Kael, speaking about Robert Redford

- 'He has so many fish hooks in his nose, he looks like a piece of bait.'
  Sports commentator Bob Costas, speaking about basketball star Dennis Rodman

- 'He has the vocal modulation of a railway-station announcer, the expressive power of a fencepost and the charisma of a week-old head of lettuce.'
  Film critic Fintan O'Toole, speaking about Quentin Tarantino

- 'I think Mick Jagger would be astounded and amazed if he realised to how many people he is not a sex symbol but a mother image.'
  David Bowie

- 'Elvis transcends his talent to the point of dispensing with it altogether.'
  Rock music critic Greil Marcus, speaking about Elvis Presley

- 'He sounds like he's got a brick dangling from his willy, and a food-mixer making purée of his tonsils.'
  Musician Paul Lester, speaking about Jon Bon Jovi

INSULTS

- 'Pamela Lee said her name is tattooed on her husband's penis. Which explains why she changed her name from Anderson to Lee.'
  US talk-show host Conan O'Brien, speaking about ex-Mötley Crüe drummer Tommy Lee

- 'Presley sounded like Jayne Mansfield looked – blowsy and loud and low.'
  Columnist Julie Burchill, speaking about Elvis Presley

- 'He looks like a dwarf who's been dipped in a bucket of pubic hair.'
  British musician Boy George, speaking about Prince

- 'Sleeping with George Michael would be like having sex with a groundhog.'
  Boy George

- 'If ignorance ever goes to $40 a barrel, I want drilling rights on George Bush's head.'
  Columnist and author Jim Hightower

- 'A pin-stripin' polo-playin' umbrella-totin' Ivy-Leaguer, born with a silver spoon so far in his mouth that you couldn't get it out with a crowbar.'
  Former Alabama Attorney General Bill Baxley, speaking about George Bush

———— INSULTS ————

- 'He can't help it – he was born with a silver foot in his mouth.'
  Former Texas Governor Ann Richards, speaking about George Bush

- 'He's a Boy Scout with a hormone imbalance.'
  Political analyst Kevin Phillips, speaking about George Bush

- 'He would kill his own mother just so that he could use her skin to make a drum to beat his own praises.'
  Society figure and wit Margot Asquith, speaking about Winston Churchill

- 'Bill Clinton's foreign policy experience is pretty much confined to having had breakfast once at the International House of Pancakes.'
  Republican Pat Buchanan

- 'He is a shifty-eyed goddamn liar... He's one of the few in the history of this country to run for high office talking out of both sides of his mouth at the same time, and lying out of both sides.'
  Harry Truman, speaking about Richard Nixon

- 'Clinton is a man who thinks international affairs means dating a girl from out of town.'
  Best-selling author Tom Clancy

INSULTS

- 'He doesn't die his hair – he's just prematurely orange.'
  Gerald Ford, speaking about Ronald Reagan

- 'He is so dumb, he can't fart and chew gum at the same time.'
  Lyndon Baines Johnson, speaking about Gerald Ford

- 'Avoid all needle drugs – the only dope worth shooting is Richard Nixon.'
  Abbie Hoffman, 1960s counter-culture icon

- 'Nixon's motto was: If two wrongs don't make a right, try three.'
  Editor and writer Norman Cousins, speaking about Richard Nixon

- 'When he does smile, he looks as if he's just evicted a widow.'
  Pulitzer Prize-winning columnist Mike Royko, speaking about former presidential candidate Bob Dole

- 'Dan Quayle is more stupid than Ronald Reagan put together.'
  The Simpsons creator Matt Groening

- 'That's not writing, that's typing.'
  US author Truman Capote, commenting on Jack Kerouac's style

INSULTS

- 'He inherited some good instincts from his Quaker forebears, but by diligent hard work, he overcame them.'
  Author James Reston, speaking about Richard Nixon

- 'I may not know much, but I know chicken shit from chicken salad.'
  Lyndon Baines Johnson, commenting on a speech by Richard Nixon

- 'President Clinton apparently gets so much action that every couple of weeks they have to spray WD-40 on his zipper.'
  US talk-show host David Letterman

- 'If life were fair, Dan Quayle would be making a living asking, "Do you want fries with that?"'
  British actor and comedian John Cleese

- 'He doesn't die his hair, he bleaches his face.'
  US talk-show host Johnny Carson, speaking about Ronald Reagan

- 'The stupid person's idea of the clever person.'
  Irish writer Elizabeth Bowen, speaking about Aldous Huxley

- 'The only time he opens his mouth is to change feet.'
  Golf commentator David Feherty, speaking about Nick Faldo

--- **INSULTS** ---

- 'I think Nancy does most of his talking; you'll notice that she never drinks water when Ronnie speaks.'
  US actor and comedian Robin Williams, speaking about Ronald Reagan

- 'Washington could not tell a lie; Nixon could not tell the truth; Reagan cannot tell the difference.'
  US comic Mort Sahl

- 'Once he makes up his mind, he's full of indecision.'
  US pianist and actor Oscar Levant, speaking about Dwight D Eisenhower

- 'The world is rid of him, but the deadly slime of his touch remains.'
  English painter John Constable, commenting on the death of Lord Byron

- 'He was a great friend of mine. Well, as much as you could be a friend of his, unless you were a 14-year-old nymphet.'
  US author Truman Capote, speaking about William Faulkner

- 'The last time I was in Spain I got through six Jeffrey Archer novels. I must remember to take enough toilet paper next time.'
  Comic Bob Monkhouse

INSULTS

- 'Nothing but old fags and cabbage-stumps of quotations from the Bible and the rest, stewed in the juice of deliberate, journalistic dirty-mindedness.'
  D H Lawrence, speaking about James Joyce

- 'Once you've put one of his books down, you simply can't pick it up again.'
  Mark Twain, speaking about Henry James

- 'What other culture could have produced someone like Hemingway and not seen the joke?'
  Author and columnist Gore Vidal

- 'Dr Donne's verses are like the peace of God; they pass all understanding.'
  James I

- 'There are two ways of disliking poetry; one way is to dislike it, the other is to read Pope.'
  Oscar Wilde, speaking about Alexander Pope

- 'That insolent little ruffian, that crapulous lout. When he quitted a sofa, he left behind him a smear.'
  Poet Norman Cameron, speaking about Dylan Thomas

- 'Reading him is like wading through glue.'
  Lord Alfred Tennyson, speaking about Ben Johnson

INSULTS

- 'They told me that Gladstone read Homer for fun, which I thought served him right.'
  Winston Churchill

- 'Elizabeth Taylor has more chins than the Chinese telephone directory.'
  Joan Rivers

- 'I have more talent in my smallest fart than you have in your entire body.'
  Walter Matthau to Barbra Streisand

- 'He has a face like a warthog that has been stung by a wasp.'
  Golf commentator David Feherty, speaking about Colin Montgomerie

- 'The only person who ever left the Iron Curtain wearing it.'
  US actor and pianist Oscar Levant, speaking about Zsa Zsa Gabor

- 'She ran the whole gamut of emotions from A to B.'
  Dorothy Parker, speaking about Katharine Hepburn

- 'You can calculate Zsa Zsa Gabor's age by the rings on her fingers.'
  Bob Hope

INSULTS

● 'The plain truth is, that he was a most intolerable ruffian, a disgrace to human nature, and a blot of blood and grease upon the history of England.'
Charles Dickens, speaking about Henry VIII

● 'He writes his plays for the ages – the ages between five and twelve.'
US author George Nathan, speaking about George Bernard Shaw

● 'Sarah Brightman couldn't act scared on the New York subway at 4 o'clock in the morning.'
Film-maker Joel Segal, speaking about theatre actress Sarah Brightman

● 'Zsa Zsa Gabor has been married so many times, she has rice marks on her face.'
US comic and actor Henry Youngman

● 'She has breasts of granite and a mind like a Gruyère cheese.'
Film-maker Billy Wilder, speaking about Marilyn Monroe

● 'Martina was so far in the closet, she was in danger of being a garment bag.'
Lesbian author Rita Mae Brown, speaking about tennis star Martina Navratilova

INSULTS

- 'Joan always cries a lot. Her tear ducts must be close to her bladder.'
  Bette Davis, speaking about Joan Crawford

- 'She speaks five languages and can't act in any of them.'
  John Gielgud, speaking about Ingrid Bergman

- 'She looks like she combs her hair with an eggbeater.'
  Columnist Louella Parsons, speaking about Joan Collins

- 'A woman whose face looked as if it had been made of sugar and someone had licked it.'
  George Bernard Shaw, speaking about dancer Isadora Duncan

- 'Hah! I always knew Frank would end up in bed with a boy!'
  Actress Ava Gardner, speaking about Mia Farrow's marriage to her ex-husband Frank Sinatra

- 'Elizabeth Taylor's so fat, she puts mayonnaise on aspirin.'
  US comic Joan Rivers

- 'The only genius with an IQ of 60.'
  Author and columnist Gore Vidal, speaking about Andy Warhol

- 'She's a vacuum with nipples.'
  Film-maker Otto Preminger, speaking about Marilyn Monroe

INSULTS

- 'Nowadays a parlour maid as ignorant as Queen Victoria was when she came to the throne would be classed as mentally defective.'
  George Bernard Shaw, speaking about Queen Victoria

- 'Dramatic art in her opinion is knowing how to fill a sweater.'
  Bette Davis, speaking about Jayne Mansfield

- 'It's a new low for actresses when you have to wonder what's between her ears instead of her legs.'
  Katharine Hepburn, speaking about Sharon Stone

- 'The closest thing to Roseanne Barr's singing the national anthem was my cat being neutered.'
  US talk-show host Johnny Carson

- 'When it comes to acting, Joan Rivers has the range of a wart.'
  Author Stewart Klein

- 'She is closer to organised prostitution than anything else.'
  Singer Morrissey, speaking about Madonna

- 'Comparing Madonna with Marilyn Monroe is like comparing Raquel Welch to the back of a bus.'
  Boy George

INSULTS

- 'A cross between an aardvark and an albino rat.'
  Film critic John Simon, speaking about Barbra Streisand

- 'I didn't know her well, but after watching her in action
  I didn't want to know her well.'
  Joan Crawford, speaking about Judy Garland

- 'Her voice sounded like an eagle being goosed.'
  Author Ralph Novak, speaking about Yoko Ono

- 'If I found her floating in my pool, I'd punish my dog.'
  US comic Joan Rivers, speaking about Yoko Ono

- 'A senescent bimbo with a lust for home furnishings.'
  *Author and social critic Barbara Ehrenreich, speaking about
  Nancy Reagan*

- 'In her last days, she resembled a spoiled pear.'
  *Author and columnist Gore Vidal, speaking about US
  experimental writer Gertrude Stein*

- 'She looks like something that would eat its young.'
  Dorothy Parker, speaking about actress Dame Edith Evans

- 'Virginia Woolf's writing is no more than glamorous
  knitting. I believe she must have a pattern somewhere.'
  Poet Dame Edith Sitwell, speaking about Virginia Woolf

INSULTS

- 'She looked like a huge ball of fur on two well-developed legs.'
  Novelist Nancy Mitford, speaking about Princess Margaret

- 'A fungus of pendulous shape.'
  Writer Alice James, speaking about George Eliot

- 'I am fairly unrepentant about her poetry. I really think that three quarters of it is gibberish. However, I must crush down these thoughts, otherwise the dove of peace will shit on me.'
  Noel Coward, speaking about poet Dame Edith Sitwell

- 'Every word she writes is a lie, including "and" and "the".'
  US writer and critic Mary McCarthy, speaking about US playwright and memoirist Lillian Hellman

6

THE HUMAN BODY

DEVELOPMENT

- Children born in the month of May are, on average, 200 g heavier at birth than children born in any other month.

- The weight of a foetus increases by about 2.4 billion times in nine months.

- A human foetus acquires fingerprints at the age of three months.

- A four-month-old foetus will startle and turn away if a bright light is flashed on its mother's belly. Babies in the womb will also react to sudden loud noises, even if their mother's ears are muffled.

- Newborn babies are not blind, with newborns having approximately 20/50 vision, and can easily discriminate between degrees of brightness.

- Most newborns cry without tears until they are three to six weeks old.

- A newborn baby's head accounts for about one-quarter of its entire weight.

- The 'spring up, fall out' phenomenon claims that children grow twice as fast in the spring as they do in the autumn (fall), while they gain more weight in autumn.

―――――――――― **DEVELOPMENT** ――――――――――

- Babies have the strongest sense of smell, enabling them to recognise their mothers by scent.

- A boy's voice breaks during puberty because his vocal cords are lengthening. Up until that point, girls' and boys' vocal cords are the same length.

- Up to the age of six or seven months, a child can breathe and swallow at the same time, unlike an adult.

- Babies like pretty faces better than plain ones.

- In toddlers, most non-food-related choking accidents are caused by balloons (29%), and balls and marbles (19%). Older children are more likely to die from balloons than are toddlers.

- Six-year-olds laugh an average of 300 times a day. Adults only laugh 15 to 100 times a day.

- The common cold will delay a child's growth for the duration of the cold.

- Following a family move, boys between the ages of six and 11 tend to have problems adjusting to new environments, particularly school. Indeed, moving may be so potentially traumatic for that age group as to cause

------------------ **DEVELOPMENT** ------------------

a drop in academic achievement or even IQ. The results were not conclusive for girls.

- About 25% of all children have one or more sleepwalking episodes between the ages of seven and twelve.

- Until about age 12, boys cry about as often as girls.

- Allergies cause students in the United States to miss 1.5 million school days a year, with these allergy sufferers experiencing a significantly reduced ability to learn.

———— DISEASE AND TREATMENTS ————

● Throughout history, the most destructive disease is malaria. More than 1.5 million people die from malaria every year.

● The Spanish flu was unlike most flu viruses, as it hit the young and healthy hardest. The pandemic killed 20 million to 40 million people in 1918. Comparatively, about 13 million died in the battles of World War I.

● There are more than 100 different viruses that cause the common cold.

● In ancient Rome, gold salves were used for the treatment of skin ulcers. Today, gold leaf plays an important role in the treatment of chronic ulcers.

● In medieval Europe, alchemists mixed powdered gold into drinks to 'comfort sore limbs', one of the earliest references to arthritis.

● In the latter part of the 18th century, Prussian surgeons treated stutterers by snipping off portions of their tongues.

---------------------- MUSCLES ----------------------

- The average male adult can bench-press 88% of his body weight, having between 70 and 80 lb (32–36 kg) of muscle.

- The average man's muscles comprise about 40% of body weight, or about 70 lb (32 kg). The average woman's muscles make up about 30% of body weight, or about 43 lb (20 kg).

- It requires the use of 72 muscles to speak a single word.

- It takes 17 facial muscles to smile, but 42 to frown.

- Muscles can shorten themselves, but cannot lengthen themselves. Every time a muscle contracts, it must be pulled back to its original length by another muscle shortening itself in the other direction.

- Today, American dentists use some 13 tons of gold each year for crowns, bridges, inlays and dentures. This is because gold is non-toxic, can be shaped easily, and is tough – it never wears, corrodes, or tarnishes.

- False teeth are often radioactive. Approximately one million Americans wear some form of denture; half of these dentures are made of a porcelain compound laced with minute amounts of uranium to stimulate

MUSCLES

fluorescence. Without the uranium additive, the dentures would be a dull green colour when seen under artificial light.

- The average American adult male brushes his teeth 1.9 times a day.

- Tooth enamel is the hardest substance manufactured by the human body.

─────────── **BONES AND SKELETONS** ───────────

- The strongest bone in the body, the thigh bone, is hollow. Ounce for ounce, it has a greater pressure tolerance and bearing strength than a rod of equivalent size in cast steel.

- There are 22 bones in the adult human skull.

- Of the 206 bones in the average adult human body, 106 are found in the hands and feet (54 are in the hands, 52 are in the feet).

- Human bones can withstand being squeezed twice as hard as granite can. Bones can also stand being stretched four times as hard as concrete can.

- Human bones can withstand stresses of 24,000 lb per square inch (16,873,670 kg/m^2).

- When astronauts remain weightless in space for prolonged periods, scientists have discovered their bones lose a measurable amount of weight and thickness. This means that weightlessness actually causes human beings to shrink.

- The mineral content, porosity, and general make-up of human bone is nearly identical to some species of South Pacific coral. The two are so alike that plastic surgeons

BONES AND SKELETONS

are using the coral in facial reconstructions, to replace lost human bone.

- From birth to adolescence, selected bones in the human body fuse together. The last bone to fuse is the collarbone, and this occurs between the ages of 18 and 25.

SKIN, SWEAT AND BACTERIA

- The average person sheds about 1 1/2 lb (about 0.7 kg) of skin each year.

- The skin of the armpits can harbour up to 516,000 bacteria per square inch (about 172,000 per square centimetre), while drier areas, such as the forearm, have only about 13,000 bacteria per square inch (about 4,000 per square centimetre).

- The average person's total skin covering would weigh about 6 lb (about 3 kg) if collected in one mass.

- If the skin of a 150-lb (68 kg) person were spread out flat, it would cover approximately 20 square feet (about 1.9 m²).

- A human can detect the wing of a bee falling on his or her cheek from a height of 1 cm.

- There are approximately 250,000 sweat glands in your feet, and they sweat as much as 8 oz (0.2 litres) of moisture per day.

- The skin is only about as deep as the tip of a ballpoint pen.

- There are about two million sweat glands in the average human body. The average adult loses 540 calories with every litre of sweat. Men sweat about 40% more than women.

———— SKIN, SWEAT AND BACTERIA ————

- Around one-third of all faeces is solid bacteria.

- There are more bacteria in your mouth than there are people in the world.

- An average man, on an average day, excretes 2 $\frac{1}{2}$ quarts (2.8 litres) of sweat.

- The bacteria found on human skin are roughly the numerical equivalent of all the humans on earth.

- Ten per cent of your body weight would be from micro-organisms on your body if you were freeze-dried.

- Sweat itself is odourless. Only when combined with bacteria that are breaking down dead skin cells does it smell. Smelly sweat is called 'bromhidrosis'. Sweat is composed of water, sodium chloride, potassium salts, urea and lactic acid.

- The palms of the hands and soles of the feet contain more sweat glands than any other part of the body.

- First-degree burns affect only the very top layers of the skin. Second-degree burns penetrate midway through the skin's thickness. Third-degree burns penetrate and damage the entire thickness of the skin.

TEETH

- According to a report in *Dentistry*, scientists have estimated that speech involves at least 100 muscles. In normal speaking, we make about 14 sounds per second. Therefore, when speaking, we generate 1,400 neuromuscular events per second.

- If one identical twin grows up without a given tooth coming in, the second identical twin will usually also grow up without the tooth.

BRAIN

- The average brain comprises 2% of a person's total body weight. Yet it requires 25% of all oxygen used by the body, as opposed to 12% used by the kidneys and 7% by the heart.

- There are 100 billion neurons in the human brain with each neuron linked to hundreds of others.

- In one day, the human brain generates more electrical impulses than all the telephones in the world put together. The nerve impulses can travel as fast as 170 mph (274 kph).

- Man's 3-lb (1.3 kg) brain is the most complex and orderly arrangement of matter known in the universe.

- The brain is not sensitive to pain. Headache pain originates in the nerves, muscles, and tissues surrounding the skull, not from the brain. If it is cut into, the person feels no pain.

- The brain of Neanderthal man was larger than that of modern man, with a capacity 100 cc larger than modern man's.

- The human brain is greyish pink in colour and has a texture much like tofu.

BRAIN

- On average, a woman's brain makes up 2.5% of her body weight. A man's brain only contributes 2% of his body weight.

- The human brain continues sending out electrical wave signals for up to 37 hours following death.

- The human brain is capable of recording over 86 million bits of information daily.

- Your brain is more active sleeping than it is watching TV.

- The left hemisphere of the brain controls language in 95% of right-handed people. In left-handed people, 70% have language controlled by the right hemisphere.

- Brain-wave activity in humans changes when we catch the punchline of a joke.

- The short-term memory capacity for most people is between five and nine items or digits. This is one reason that phone numbers were kept to seven digits (not including area code).

———— EYES AND EYESIGHT ————

- A bird's eye takes up about 50% of its head; the human eye takes up about 5% of the head. To be comparable to a bird's eyes, the eyes of a human being would have to be the size of baseballs.

- Visual scientists have estimated that, by the age of 60, our eyes have been exposed to more light energy than would be released by a nuclear blast.

- The average adult eyeball weighs about 1 oz (about 28 g).

- The average duration of a single blink of the human eye is 0.3 seconds.

- The average human eye can distinguish about 500 different shades of grey.

- The average human eyelash lives about 150 days.

- There are 1,200,000 fibres in a human optic nerve.

- The average person's field of vision encompasses a 200°-wide angle.

- The iris of the human eye provides better identification than a fingerprint. A scan of the iris has 256 different unique characteristics. A fingerprint has only forty.

EYES AND EYESIGHT

- The human eyes can perceive more than one million simultaneous visual impressions and are able to discriminate among nearly eight million gradations of colour.

- The average time between blinks of the eye is 2.8 seconds.

- Uncontrollable winking is the physical symptom of those suffering from 'blepharospasms'.

- We think we cannot see at night. But given enough time to adjust, the human eye can, for a time, see almost as well as an owl's. Ultimately, as the amount of light decreases, an owl detects shapes after a human no longer can.

- It takes the human eyes an hour to adapt completely to seeing in the dark. Once adapted, however, the eyes are about 100,000 times more sensitive to light than they are in bright sunlight.

- While seven men in 100 have some form of colour blindness, only one woman in 1,000 suffers from it. The most common form of colour blindness is a red-green deficiency.

——— EYES AND EYESIGHT ———

- The lens of the eye continues to grow throughout a person's life.

- The human eye is continuously but imperceptibly moving. Muscle contractions cause it to quiver 30 to 50 times per second.

- Sight accounts for 90 to 95% of all sensory perceptions.

- While reading a page of print, the eyes do not move continually across the page. They move in a series of jumps, called 'fixations', from one clump of words to the next.

- You blink every two to 10 seconds. As you focus on each word in this sentence, your eyes swing back and forth 100 times a second; every second, the retina performs 10 billion computer-like calculations.

- Among a sampling of American seventh-graders who were given the SAT test, 55% of the children who did 'exceptionally well' on either the maths or verbal sections were short-sighted.

- Some totally blind people can somehow sense light, explaining what keeps some blind people's biological rhythms in sync with that of sighted people's.

EYES AND EYESIGHT

- The only part of the human body that has no blood supply is the cornea. It takes its oxygen directly from the air.

- The pupil of the eye expands as much as 45% when a person looks at something pleasing.

- The retina of the eye – thinner than a postage stamp and no larger than a ten-pence piece – can perceive and dissolve a new image every tenth of a second.

- The sensitivity of the human eye is so keen that on a clear, moonless night, a person standing on a mountain can see a match being struck as far as 50 miles (80 km) away. Much to their amazement, astronauts in orbit were able to see the wakes of ships.

- When you have a black eye, you have a 'bilateral periorbital haematoma'.

- 'Strabismus' is the condition of a person's eyes going in different directions.

DIGESTION, WEIGHT AND FAT

- The average female between the ages of 20 and 44 is more likely to be overweight than are males in the same age category.

- There is evidence that many people gain and lose weight in accordance with the cycles of the moon.

- Just sitting and doing nothing, the average person burns 1,700 calories of energy, or 7,000 kilojoules.

- The most obese people in the world are in Russia (25.4%), followed by Mexico (25.1%). Obesity is defined as 30 lb (14 kg) or more over a healthy weight.

- On an average day, the average adult spends 77 minutes eating.

- A person would have to play ping-pong for 12 hours to burn enough calories to lose 1 lb (0.4536 kg).

- The average adult has between 40 and 50 billion fat cells.

- A person is more likely to eat twice as much in the company of others as when eating alone.

- The richer the food you eat, the longer it takes to leave the stomach.

DIGESTION, WEIGHT AND FAT

- The average woman consumes 2,000 calories a day, the average man about 2,500. However, if you had the metabolism of a shrew, you would need to consume about 200,000 calories a day. Metabolic rate is the sum of all the chemical reactions occurring in the body at one time. The faster the reactions, the higher your metabolism and the more calories you need to consume. Smaller animals tend to have higher metabolic rates because they have to work harder to keep their bodies warm.

- The hydrochloric acid of the human digestive process is so strong a corrosive that it easily can eat its way through a cotton handkerchief, and even through the iron of a car body. Yet, it doesn't endanger the stomach's sticky mucus walls.

- Medical experts warn that compulsive exercising can be just as bad for a person as no exercise at all. The human body needs 24 hours without exercise about once a week in order to cleanse itself of lactic acid and other waste products of strenuous activity.

- According to acupuncturists, there is a point on the head that you can press to control your appetite. It is located in the hollow just in front of the flap of the ear.

- The average digestive tract of an adult is 30 ft (9 m) in length.

EARS AND HEARING

- The sound of a snore (up to 69 decibels) can be almost as loud as the noise of a pneumatic drill (70–90 decibels).

- The easiest sounds for the human ear to hear, and those which carry best when pronounced, are (in order): 'ah', 'aw', 'eh' and 'oo'.

- Normal hearing can detect sounds as soft as 10 decibels and as loud as 140 decibels.

- When a person dies, hearing is generally the last sense to go. The first sense lost is usually sight. Then follows taste, smell and touch.

- The human ear can distinguish more than 1,500 different musical tones.

- A human can hear the tick of a watch from 6 metres in very quiet conditions.

- Loud talk can be 10 times more distracting than the sound of a jackhammer. Loud, incessant chatter can make a listener nervous and irritable, and even start him on the road to insanity.

- If your hearing is normal, you can hear sounds as deep as 20 Hz and as high as 20,000 Hz.

———————— HEART AND BLOOD ————————

- Cutting off the blood supply to the brain causes a loss of consciousness in 10 seconds, with death occurring within minutes.

- The substance that human blood resembles most closely in terms of chemical composition is seawater.

- The average healthy person can lose as much as one-third of his or her blood without fatal results.

- There is a subtype of blood called A–H, but to date, only three people in the world are known to have it.

- In one year, the average human heart circulates between 3,500,489 and 7,273,744 litres of blood through the body. This is enough fluid to fill 200 tankers, each with a capacity of 36,369 litres.

- The average human heart beats about 100,000 times every 24 hours. In a 72-year lifetime, the heart beats more than 2.5 billion times.

- Two hundred beats per minute is the maximum heartbeat possible for a human.

- In one hour, your heart produces enough energy to raise almost 1 ton (1,016 kg) of weight a yard (0.9 m) off the

—————— **HEART AND BLOOD** ——————

ground, and it beats 40,000,000 times in a year.

- A baby's heart is one-sixteenth the size of an adult's, but contains the same number of cells.

- In the second it takes to turn the page of a book, you will lose about three million red blood cells. During that same second, your bone marrow will have produced the same number of new ones.

- A simple, moderately severe sunburn damages the blood vessels to such an extent that it takes from 4 to 15 months for them to return to their normal condition.

- It has been medically proven that pessimism raises blood pressure. The more pessimistic a person is, the more likely he or she is to die earlier than optimistic counterparts.

- It takes only 15 watts of electricity going through a human body to stop the heart. Common light bulbs run on about 25 to 75 watts of electricity.

- The human heart grows by enlargement of cells, not cell multiplication.

- The valves of the human heart are as thick as a single piece of tissue paper.

——— HEART AND BLOOD ———

- If all the blood vessels in a single human body were stretched end to end, they would form a string capable of going around the world.

- The human heart rests between beats. In an average lifetime of 70 years, the total resting time is estimated to be about 40 years.

- The human heart is no bigger than a fist and yet is wrapped in so much muscle that it can continue pumping, even if a third of its muscle mass is destroyed.

- If laid out in a straight line, the average adult's circulatory system would be nearly 60,000 miles (96,558 km) long – enough to circle Earth two and a half times.

- The heart beats faster during a brisk walk or a heated argument than during sexual intercourse.

TONGUE & TASTE

- The average lifespan of a human being's taste bud is 7 to 10 days.

- The average human has about 10,000 taste buds, but they're not all on the tongue. Some are under the tongue; some are on the inside of the cheeks; some are on the roof of the mouth; and some can even be found on the lips – these are especially sensitive to salt.

- The human tongue registers bitter tastes 10,000 times more strongly than sweet tastes.

- A human tongue tastes bitter things towards the back. Salty and pungent flavours are detected at the middle of the tongue, sweet flavours at the tip.

- A human can taste 1 g of salt in 500 litres of water (0.0001M).

- Humans, if they are very sensitive to taste, can detect sweetness in a solution of 1 part sugar to 200 parts water. Some moths and butterflies can detect sweetness when the ratio is 1 to 300,000.

- Pigs, dogs and some other animals can taste water, but people cannot. Humans don't actually taste the water; they taste the chemicals and impurities in the water.

——————— HANDS AND NAILS ———————

- The thumbnail grows the slowest; the middle nail grows the fastest.

- The fingernails grow faster on the hand you favour. If you are right-handed then your right fingernails will grow faster; likewise the fingernails on the left hand of a left-handed person.

- Our nails grow at 0.1 mm per day. It takes about three months to replace one entire fingernail.

─── MISCELLANEOUS ───

- The average adult stands 0.4 in (1 cm) taller in the morning than in the evening, because the cartilage in the spine compresses during the day.

- We filter out 99% of the sights, sounds and other sensations around us if they don't seem threatening or important. If we didn't filter, the sensory overload would drive us insane.

- The average human body holds enough sulphur to kill all the fleas on an average dog, enough potassium to fire a toy cannon, enough carbon to make 900 pencils, enough fat to make 7 bars of soap, 10 gallons (45 litres) of water and enough phosphorous to make 2,200 match heads.

- The average human liver is more than five times the weight of the human heart.

- The average person can live up to 11 days without water, assuming a mean temperature of 60°F (15°C).

- In the past 10 years, organ donors have saved more lives and improved the quality of living for more Americans than the United States lost in the Korean and Vietnam wars combined.

- One brow wrinkle is the result of 200,000 frowns.

---------------- **MISCELLANEOUS** ----------------

- Ulcers seem to be aggravated more by decaffeinated coffee than by regular coffee.

- In the time it takes to read this sentence, 50,000 cells in your body will die and be replaced with new cells.

- The average able person will walk 115,000 miles (185,070 km) in their lifetime, or around the world 4 $^1/_2$ times.

- In the afternoon, your feet are bigger than at any other time of the day.

- The average life span of a fifth-century man in England was 30 years.

- The average life span of an ancient Greek or Roman man was 36 years.

- The average person takes between 8,000 and 10,000 steps a day.

- Twins are born less frequently in the eastern part of the world than in the western.

- Whispering is more wearing on your voice than a normal speaking tone. Whispering and shouting stretch the vocal cords.

MISCELLANEOUS

- People who attend church, synagogue, or other religious services once a week live to an average age of 82. Non-churchgoers live to an average age of 75, or seven years less.

- Man has tiny bones once meant for a tail and unworkable muscles once meant to move his ears.

- The body's daily requirement of vitamins and minerals is less than a thimbleful.

- Midgets and dwarfs almost always have normal-sized children, even if both parents are midgets or dwarfs.

- More than four million artificial body parts have been installed in Americans.

- Most people's legs are slightly different lengths.

- The fastest sneeze recorded travelled at 103.6 mph (166.7 kph).

- When walking, the weight of an average adult puts a downward pressure of 12,000 lb per square inch (8,436,835 kg/m^2) on each thighbone. In this case, even the thinnest part of the thighbone, at one inch (2.5 cm) thick, bears the weight of a male African elephant.

—————— MISCELLANEOUS ——————

- No one truly has double joints. Contortionists are actually able to stretch the fibrous tissues known as ligaments.

- One individual organ transplant donor can provide organs, bone, and tissue for 50 or more people in need.

- Only one person in two billion will live to be 116 or older.

- Ninety-eight per cent of all acute sunstroke cases are fatal.

- Pain travels at a speed of 350 ft (107 m) per second.

- The human spinal cord reaches its full length by the time you are four or five years old.

- A number of plastic surgeons now require their prospective patients to undergo a series of psychological tests to determine if they will become emotionally unstable, excessively anxious, or threatening to the doctor following their cosmetic surgery.

- The National Institute of Mental Health places fear of flying (aerophobia) second only to fear of public speaking.

- Two million people are hospitalised and as many as 140,000 die each year from side effects or reactions to prescription drugs.

——————— MISCELLANEOUS ———————

- The knee is the most easily injured of all the joints in the body and the most frequently treated area by orthopaedic surgeons. In America more than six million people visit an orthopaedic surgeon each year for a knee problem, with emergency rooms logging 1.4 million visits per year for knee problems.

- For more than 100,000 years, the maximum human life span has been 120 years.

- Anthropologists use a standard height of 4 ft 11 inches (1.5m) to determine if a group of people are pygmies. The average adult male must be less than 59 inches (150 cm) in height to be considered as such.

- The number of centenarians – 100 years and older – has more than doubled since 1980 to about 50,000. Four in five were women.

- A recent study found that 75% of headache patients felt relief when they rubbed capsaicin (the compound that makes chilli peppers hot) on their nose.

- A sense of humour was dependent on nurture, not nature, discovered British scientists. Their study involved 71 pairs of identical twins and 56 pairs of fraternal twins, and analysed their reactions to five drawings by

—————— MISCELLANEOUS ——————

cartoonist Gary Larson. Results showed that the siblings had similar views about the cartoons, and that the identical twins, who have the same genes, were no more likely than fraternal twins to find the same things amusing.

- At Tokyo's Keio University Hospital, 30% of the outpatients diagnosed with throat polyps attributed the cause of the affliction to singing karaoke.

- The loss of just 15% of the body's water can be fatal.

- The spinal cord is as flexible as a rubber hose.

- Snakes top the phobia list for people, at 25%, followed by a fear of being buried alive, at 22%.

- People who lose a friend, relative or loved one through death face great physical risks. They are 14 times more likely than normal to suffer a heart attack the day after the death; two days after the traumatic event, they are at risk five times more than normal.

- The period between the hours of four and six in the afternoon is when people are the most irritable. Evidence has shown that more human bites are treated in hospitals at this time of the day than at any other.

MISCELLANEOUS

- An adult human head weighs about 12 lb (5.4 kg), or the same as a light bowling ball.

- Even if the stomach, the spleen, 75% of the liver, 80% of the intestines, one kidney, one lung, and virtually every organ from the pelvic and groin area are removed, the human body can still survive.

- All humans are born with the reflexes for shivering, urination and the knee-jerk reaction when the tendon below the knee is tapped.

- One in 11 people suffer from some kind of phobia at some time in their lives. Psychologists know little about the origin of phobias.

- Between ages 30 and 70, a nose may lengthen and widen by as much as half an inch (1.3 cm) and the ears may be a quarter of an inch (0.6 cm) longer. This occurs because cartilage is one of the few tissues that continues to grow as we age.

- The colour light green is effective in relieving the feelings of homesickness.

- Sex, angry outbursts and strenuous tennis are among the triggers identified as responsible for 17% of all heart attacks.

MISCELLANEOUS

- Scientists estimate that they could fill a 1,000-volume encyclopaedia with the coded instructions in the DNA of a single human cell if the instructions could be translated into English.

- Pound for pound, the human body produces more heat than the sun. The sun's heat production averages only two calories per pound of its mass daily, while the average human body generates 10 calories per pound of mass each day – five times as much as the sun.

- Hiccups are caused by a sudden contraction of the diaphragm, which drags air into the lungs so fast that it snaps the vocal cords shut.

- Events such as pleasant family celebrations or evenings with friends boost the immune system for the following two days. Unpleasant moments have the opposite effect: negative events, such as being criticised at work, were found to weaken the immune function for one day afterward.

- A baby girl is born with thousands of egg cells already in her ovaries.

- Seeing another person yawn makes it likely that you will yawn yourself. Thinking about or even reading about

——————— MISCELLANEOUS ———————

yawning can set you off. People with mental disorders such as psychoses rarely yawn.

- If 80% of your liver were to be removed, the remaining part would continue to function. Within a few months, the liver would have reconstituted itself to its original size.

- The rush of air produced by a cough moves at a speed approaching 600 mph (966 kph).

- Some psychologists contend that many people enjoy anxiety, owing to the popularity of horror films and roller coasters.

- Sometimes a baby is born with one or two of its first teeth already present.

- Men's brains are less well formed and shrink at a faster rate than women's.

- Stress may be good for people. Rockefeller University scientists have determined that an acute episode of stress boosts immunity, offering better protection against infection.

- If you are right-handed, you will tend to chew your food on the right side of the mouth. If you are left-handed, you will tend to chew your food on the left.

MISCELLANEOUS

- Fingers and toes get wrinkled like prunes when you soak them in water too long because the skin cells have absorbed some of the water. Fingers, toes and the soles of feet are covered in a thick layer of tough skin. When it absorbs the water; the skin on these body parts has nowhere to expand to, so it buckles into wrinkles.

- As babies develop in the uterus, their bodies are covered in fine, downy hair called lanugo, which usually disappears before they are born.

- To keep a corpse's lips shut, undertakers pass a suture through the nasal septum and tie it to the lower lip, or use an injector needle gun to place wires into the lower and upper jaws; these are then twisted together to close the mouth.

- Staying warm in cold weather isn't easy. Up to 1,800 calories daily – 90% of many people's energy intake – may have to be burned to maintain a body temperature of 98.6°F (37°C).

- The average person takes between 12 and 18 breaths per minute.

- If you never get thirsty, you need to drink more water. When the human body is dehydrated, its thirst mechanism shuts off.

—————————— MISCELLANEOUS ——————————

- Undertakers report that human bodies do not deteriorate as quickly as they used to, as the modern diet contains so many preservatives that these chemicals tend to prevent the body from decomposition too rapidly after death.

- Boys are more likely to be left-handed than girls.

- If you were to unravel the entire human alimentary canal (oesophagus, stomach, large and small intestines), it would reach the height of a three-storey building.

- Muscles account for 60% of body weight.

- The first set of teeth contains 20 teeth – the 'milk' teeth.

- Some babies suck their thumb before they are born.

- Men's major body systems – the circulatory, respiratory, digestive and excretory functions – are all likely to break down long before women's.

- Puberty before the age of 10 in a boy is called 'precocious' puberty.

- Some babies, especially those with low birth weight, stop breathing for very brief periods during sleep. This is called apnoea.

BREATHING

- In one minute of breathing, the average human takes in 14 pints (6 litres) of air.

- You can't kill yourself by holding your breath. At worst, you would lose consciousness and the lungs would start to breathe automatically.

- An adult sitting in a relaxed position inhales approximately one pint of air with every breath.

- Because of their extreme elasticity, the lungs are 100 times easier to blow up than a child's toy balloon.

- The average person takes between 12 and 18 breaths per minute.

—— REPRODUCTION AND PREGNANCY ——

● Men can have eight million genetically different sperm, and women a like number of egg types. Together they can produce 64 billion children with no genetic duplicates.

● Men reach the peak of their sexual powers in their late teens or early 20s, and then slowly begin to decline. Women, however, do not reach their sexual peak until their late 20s or early 30s, and then remain at this level through their late 50s or early 60s.

● Men who take steroids to build muscle are believed to have extremely low sperm counts. After giving up steroids, it takes men one to three years to recover enough to father a child.

● Eating garlic during pregnancy can cut the risk of raised blood pressure and protein retained in the urine, or pre-eclampsia.

● The epididymis, the tube that carries spermatozoa, is 15 to 20 ft (4.5 m to 6 m) long in an adult male.

● There are fewer births nine months after a heat wave, with an increase of 12°C (53.6°F) in summer temperatures reducing births the following spring by up to 6%. This means that high temperatures could reduce people's sense of well-being, which could result in a reduction in sexual

—— REPRODUCTION AND PREGNANCY ——

interest. Similarly lower sperm counts and higher rates of miscarriage have been recorded during hot weather.

● New York men have higher sperm counts and better semen quality than Los Angeles men. Medical experts believe the warm weather and higher pollution in Los Angeles might be the culprit behind the lower counts.

● A parent's stress at the time of conception can play a major role in determining a baby's sex. The child tends to be the same sex as the parent who was under less stress.

● A man's testicles produce 72 million sperm a day – enough in six weeks to impregnate the entire world's female population.

● All the genetic material in the sperm and egg cells that produced the earth's present population could fit into a space the size of an aspirin.

● A woman's arthritic pains will almost always disappear as soon as she becomes pregnant.

● A majority of women unconsciously choose mates with a body odour that differs from their own natural scents, which, as a result, ensures better immune protection for their children.

—— REPRODUCTION AND PREGNANCY ——

- Human reproduction follows lunar time rather than sidereal, or solar, time. Gestation is about 266 days – nine lunar months – and the menstrual period is one lunar month.

- Girls born to men who are older than 50 have an average life span that is six years shorter than their brothers. Scientists believe the X, or female, chromosome a father passes to his daughter contains the gene that determines longevity.

- During menstruation, the sensitivity of a woman's middle finger is reduced.

- Women who are vegetarians may be more likely to give birth to baby girls than boys.

- Cold showers actually increase sexual arousal.

- Men are more fertile in the winter.

- Pregnancy specialists warn that using fertility drugs give couples a one-in-four chance of a multiple birth.

- Relative to its tiny size, the human sperm cell can swim 50% faster than an adult male can.

- During pregnancy, the uterus expands to 500 times its normal size.

TERMINOLOGY

- The characteristic red nose caused by broken capillaries, often caused by a person's excessive drinking over a prolonged period, is called 'rhinophyma', or 'grog blossom'.

- A 'buccula' is a little-used term for a person's double chin.

- 'Mageirocophobia' is the intense fear of having to cook.

- A 'nullipara' is a woman who has never borne a child.

- 'Zoanthropy' is a form of mental disorder in which the patient imagines himself to be a beast.

- 'Tomatophagia' is an unusual eating disorder – also known as 'pica' – and is blamed on iron deficiency anaemia. People with tomatophagia develop unusual cravings for such things as tomatoes, ice, detergent, starch, clay or even dirt.

- 'Zoonoses' are animal diseases communicable to man.

- 'Synesthesia' is a rare condition in which the senses are combined. Synesthetes see words, taste colours and shapes, and feel flavours.

- Someone with an irrational fear of meat is 'carnophobic.'

TERMINOLOGY

● 'Gymnophobia' is a fear of nakedness.

● A person who is 'scoptophobic' has an intense fear of being seen.

● If a person is 'aerophobic', they have an irrational fear of draughts.

● 'Dishabiliophobia' is a fear of undressing in front of someone.

● Someone who speaks through clenched teeth is called a 'dentiloquist'.

● If someone is 'androphobic', they have an extreme, irrational fear of men.

● If you are afraid that you might die laughing, you are suffering from 'cherophobia'.

NOSE AND SMELLING

- One-quarter of the people who lose their sense of smell also lose their desire for sexual relations.

- The human sense of smell is so keen that it can detect the odours of certain substances even when they are diluted to 1 part to 30 billion.

- Women reject heart transplants more often than men.

- A human can detect one drop of perfume diffused throughout a three-room apartment.

- By the age of 20, most humans have lost up to 20% of their sense of smell. By the age of 60, sixty per cent is gone.

- Disorders in the brain can distort odours. Epileptics sometimes get auras of strange odours just before a seizure.

MEN VERSUS WOMEN

- Women manufacture far less serotonin, the key mood-regulating brain chemical, than men. This could explain why they're more likely to suffer from certain psychological problems such as depression.

- Women navigate by landmarks and visual memories. Men navigate by direction and distance, and tend to be better at reading maps.

- The nose cleans, warms and humidifies over 500 cubic feet (14 cubic metres) of air every day.

- Blue is the colour women most prefer for bedrooms; men are happier with white bedrooms.

- Women are more prone to phobias than men.

- Only about 6% of women fail to cry at least once a month, while 50% of men fail to cry that often.

- On the average, a woman is three times more sensitive than a man to noises while sleeping.

- The average woman's thighs are one and a half times larger in circumference than the average man's.

- Men have more blood than women.

SLEEP AND DREAMS

- People dream an average of five times a night, and each subsequent dream is longer than the one preceding it. The first dream of the evening is about 10 minutes long, and the final dream lasts about 45 minutes.

- Of people who snore, 19% snore so loudly that they can be heard through a closed door.

- If the roof of your mouth is narrow, you are more prone to snore, since you are not getting enough oxygen through your nose.

- There is no one who does not dream. Those who claim to have no dreams, laboratory tests have determined, simply forget their dreams more easily than others.

- On the average, women dream more than men, and children dream more than adults. Overall, more people dream in black and white than in colour.

- As much as 6% of the world's population may experience sleep paralysis – the inability to move and speak for several minutes after awakening.

- Scientists say that people who sleep less than average (less than six hours a night) are more organised and efficient than everybody else.

7

HISTORY

HISTORY

- In America and England, witches were hanged not burnt.

- The celebration of May Day was forbidden in the time of Oliver Cromwell.

- John Hawkins began the slave trade by shipping Africans to the West Indies in the 1560s.

- St Columba and his followers first saw the Loch Ness monster in AD 565.

- The Ku Klux Klan was originally founded in the 1860s.

- The first truly humanlike creatures on earth were called Homo habilis or 'handyman'.

- To celebrate the battle of Trafalgar, a naval battle was fought on the Serpentine Lake at Hyde Park.

- The fork did not appear until the 16th century, and fork-and-knife pairs were not in general use in Britain until the 17th century.

- The first country to introduce paper money was China in 812, but it wasn't until 1661 that a bank in Sweden issued banknotes.

HISTORY

- Residential, economic, or educational qualification gave half a million Englishmen more than one vote in England in 1885. A university graduate who also owned a business in the City of London voted three times – once at his home, once for his university, and once in the City.

- Soap was considered a frivolous luxury of the British aristocracy from the early 1700s until 1862, and there was a tax on those who used it in England.

- The loudest sound that could be made in 1600 was that of a pipe organ.

- The pharaohs of ancient Egypt wore garments made with thin threads of beaten gold, with some fabrics having up to 500 gold threads per inch (2.54 cm) of cloth.

- Cockney rhyming slang began in London around the 1850s as a statement of independence felt by those who prided themselves on having been born within the sound of Bow Bells.

- In ancient Greece, courtesans wore sandals with nails studded into the sole so that their footprints would leave the message 'Follow me'.

HISTORY

- The first discovery of a South African diamond was made by children playing on a beach.

- Greenwich Mean Time only became universally accepted as the standard time throughout Britain with the growth of the railways in the late 19th century. It was felt that all train timetables should be standardised, so GMT was adopted.

- Australia gave women the vote in 1901.

- The distinctive flat-topped caps worn by the fish porters at Billingsgate market in London are said to be modelled on those worn by the English archers at the Battle of Agincourt.

- More than 100 years ago, the felt-hat-makers of England used mercury to stabilise wool, with many eventually becoming poisoned by the fumes – as demonstrated by the Mad Hatter in Lewis Carroll's *Alice in Wonderland*.

- In 1937, the emergency 999 telephone service was established in London. More than 13,000 genuine calls were made in the first month.

- The oldest city in Britain is Ripon, which received its original charter in 886.

HISTORY

- In 1060, a coin was minted in England shaped like a clover. The user could break off any of the four leaves and use them as separate pieces of currency.

- During the 16th century, platform shoes called 'chopines' became popular in Europe, with some chopines over 20 inches (50 cm) tall. In the 1400s, a popular form of shoes called 'crakows' sported extremely long toes, some over 20 inches (50 cm). The length was an indication of the social status of the person wearing them.

- In 1752, 11 days were dropped from the year when the switch from the Julian calendar to the Gregorian calendar was made. The 25 December date was effectively moved 11 days backwards. Some Christian church sects, called old calendarists, still celebrate Christmas on 7 January.

- The first contraceptive diaphragms, centuries ago, were citrus rinds.

- Obsidian balls, or occasionally brass balls, were placed in the eye sockets of Egyptian mummies.

- During the French Reign of Terror from 1793 to 1794, 500,000 people were arrested and 17,000 of them were publicly executed at the guillotine.

HISTORY

- Tangshan, in China, suffered the deadliest earthquake of the 20th century on 28 July 1976. One quarter of the population was killed or seriously injured, with an estimated 242,000 people killed.

- The population of the entire world in 5000 BC was five million.

- In World War II it cost the Allies about $225,00 to kill one enemy soldier.

- Cambridge University was established in 1209.

8

SCIENCE AND NATURE

—————— SCIENCE AND NATURE ——————

- Every power tool on the market has passed 20 safety tests.

- An energy-saving washing machine can save you enough money to buy your washing powder for six months.

- RAM stands for Random Access Memory.

- Pocket calculators first appeared in the 1970s.

- IBM is nicknamed 'Big Blue'.

- The earliest type of robot was a water clock invented in Egypt in 250 BC.

- The compact disc was developed in the 1970s.

- The first miniature TV sets appeared in the 1980s.

- Helium is the element with the lowest boiling point.

- The first Channel tunnel was started in 1877.

- Japanese cedars have bright green leaves in summer and turn purple and bronze in winter.

- Gorse and broom belong to the pea family.

SCIENCE AND NATURE

● If we were to upturn the Millennium Dome at Greenwich, it would take 3.8 billion half-litres of beer to fill it up.

● The refrigerator was first successfully developed in the 1860s.

● Halley's Comet will next appear in 2061.

● Wheeled vehicles were first invented in about 3000 BC.

● Edwin Beard Budding invented the lawnmower in 1830.

● All Model T Fords were black.

● The Mercalli scale measures the intensity of an earthquake.

● The Romans bought the sycamore tree to Britain.

● The wood at the centre of the tree stem is called heartwood.

● The kerosene fungus can live in jet fuel tanks, so if there is a minute amount of water in the tank, the fungus can use the fuel as food.

● The kowhai is the national flower of New Zealand.

SCIENCE AND NATURE

- The cedar is the national tree of Lebanon.

- Lavender takes it name from the Latin *lavare*, meaning to wash, because of its use in toilet preparations.

- Water lilies were a symbol of immortality in ancient times.

- Two objects have struck the earth with enough force to destroy a whole city. Each object, one in 1908 and again in 1947, struck regions of Siberia. Not one human being was hurt either time.

- Stitching through a piece of sandpaper is an effective way to sharpen a sewing machine needle.

- More than 45,000 pieces of plastic debris float on every square mile of ocean.

- An ounce (about 28 g) of platinum can be stretched to 10,000 ft (3,048 m).

- With 980-plus species, bats make up more than 23% of all known mammals by species.

- Nourishment, capable of sustaining life for a short time, can be gained by chewing on leather.

SCIENCE AND NATURE

- A dog can understand between 35 to 40 commands.

- The 1906 San Francisco earthquake was the equivalent of 12,000 Hiroshima nuclear bombs.

- The minimum safe distance between a wood-burning stove and flammable objects is 3 ft (0.9 m).

- More than half of the world's animal groups are found only in the sea.

- A 'hairbreadth away' is 1/48 in (0.05 cm).

- Cows can smell odours 6 miles (10 km) away.

- The average 6-month accumulation of barnacles on the hull of a ship can produce enough drag to force the vessel to burn 40% more fuel than normal when cruising.

- The world's chicken population is more than double the human population, while the world cattle population outnumbers the population of China.

- A car uses 1.6 oz (0.05 litres) of petrol idling for one minute. Half an ounce (0.015 litres) is used to start the average car.

SCIENCE AND NATURE

- A quality, fully faceted brilliant diamond has at least 58 facets.

- The average lead pencil will draw a line 35 miles (56 km) long or write approximately 50,000 English words.

- Horses can sleep standing up.

- The sun is estimated to be 20 to 21 cosmic years old.

- A 10-gallon (UK/US?) (45-litre) hat holds less than a gallon (4.5 litres) of liquid.

- The sun's warming rays travel through 93 million miles (149,664,900 km) of space to reach Earth.

- Only one polished diamond in a thousand weighs more than a carat.

- The average raindrop falls at 7 mph (11 kph).

- Other than humans, the pigs family are the only animals that can get sunburn.

- A bolt of lightning travels at speeds of up to 100 million fps (30,480,000 m/s), or 72 million mph (115,869,600 kph).

-------------- **SCIENCE AND NATURE** --------------

• Dirty snow melts faster than white snow because it's darker and absorbs more heat.

• The cargo bay of a space shuttle is large enough to hold one humpback whale, and still have room for 1,000 herrings. That's the equivalent of filling it with 250,000 4-oz chocolate bars.

• Forest fires move faster uphill than downhill.

• There are a thousand times more living things in the sea than there are on land.

• The earth weighs around 6,588,000,000,000,000,000,000,000 tons.

• A Boeing 747 jumbo jet weighs 55 times the weight of an average African elephant.

• The catfish has more taste buds than any other creature, totalling over 27,000.

• A cubic mile (4 cubic km) of ordinary fog contains less than a gallon (4.5 litres) of water.

• A US-backed government study found that pigs can become alcoholics.

——————— SCIENCE AND NATURE ———————

- Sound waves move 1,100 fps (335 m/s) in the air.

- A lightning bolt generates temperatures five times hotter than those found at the sun's surface.

- The name of the statuette atop the hood of every Rolls Royce car is 'The Spirit of Ecstasy'.

- A manned rocket reaches the moon in less time than it took a stagecoach to travel the length of Britain.

- A one-day weather forecast requires about 10 billion mathematical calculations.

- The sound of the seashore inside large seashells is the shell echoing surrounding sounds, jumbling and amplifying them.

- A balloon released into the jet stream would take two weeks to travel around the globe.

- All the land mass of the earth, plus some, could fit into the Pacific Ocean.

- A car with manual gears gets 2 miles (3 km) more per gallon (3.8 litres) of petrol than a car with automatic gears.

--------------- SCIENCE AND NATURE ---------------

- A sizeable oak tree, during the typical growing season, gives off 28,000 gallons (127,288 litres) of moisture.

- A typical lightning bolt is only 2–4 inches (5–10 cm) wide, but 2 miles (3 km) long.

- An average toilet uses 5 to 7 (19–27 litres) gallons of water every time it is flushed. A single leaky toilet can waste more than 50 (189 litres) gallons a day, amounting to 18,000 gallons (68,130 litres) a year.

- A mile on the ocean and a mile on land are not the same distance. On the ocean, a nautical mile measures 6,080 ft (1,853 m), while a land or statute mile is 5,280 ft (1,609 m).

- Crystals grow by reproducing themselves, making them the nearest to being 'alive' of all members of the mineral kingdom.

- Assuming a rate of one drop per second, a leaking tap wastes about 900 gallons (3.407 litres) of water a year.

- Glass can be made so strong that a pressure of 350 tons (356 tonnes) is required to crush a 2-in (5 cm) cube, and it can be made so fragile that the breath will break a drinking glass.

———— SCIENCE AND NATURE ————

- It takes a ton (1,016.05 kg) of ore to produce one gold wedding ring.

- Bamboo can grow by the height of a two-year-old child a day. That's 36 inches (91 cm) a day!

- Lightning is more likely than not to strike twice in the same place. Like all electric currents or discharges, lightning follows the path of least resistance.

- It takes as much heat to turn 1 oz (30 ml) of snow to water as it does to make 1 oz (30 ml) of soup boil at room temperature.

- It takes glass one million years to decompose, which means it never wears out and can be recycled an infinite amount of times.

- It has been estimated that the deep seas may contain as many as 10 million species that have yet to be discovered.

- Air pressure at sea level is roughly equal to the weight of an elephant spread over a small coffee table.

- It is estimated that 60% of home smoke detectors in use do not work because they don't have a battery in them or the battery in the detector no longer has any potency.

SCIENCE AND NATURE

- Avocado trees have collapsed under the weight of their fruit.

- Granite conducts sound 10 times faster than air.

- It takes 3,000 seeds from the giant sequoia tree to weigh one ounce (around 28 g).

- It would take 80 moons to equal the weight of the earth.

- It would take a car travelling at 100 mph (160 kph) nearly 30 million years to reach our nearest star.

- Fleas can accelerate 50 times faster than the space shuttle.

- The science of determining characteristic traits by examining a person's shoes is called 'scarpology'.

- Laptop computers get bumped around too much, which makes them around 30% more likely to fail than a computer that stays in one place.

- For every person on earth, there are 200 million insects.

- The skins of turkeys are tanned and used to make items like cowboy boots, belts and other accessories.

──────────── **SCIENCE AND NATURE** ────────────

- The hardness of ice is similar to that of concrete.

- If hot water is suddenly poured into a glass, that glass is more apt to break if it is thick than if it is thin. This is why test tubes are made of thin glass.

- A total of 7.5 million toothpicks can be produced from one cord of wood.

- Small animals like bats and shrews consume up to one and one-half times their bodyweight in food every day. For an adult male, this would be like eating 1,000 quarter-pound cheeseburgers a day, every day; or about 50 Christmas dinners a day.

- Tobacco grows from seeds so small that it takes 350,000 of them to make an ounce (around 28 g).

- If all the gold suspended in the world's seawater were mined, each person on earth would receive about 10 lb (4.5 kg).

- It's possible to lead a cow upstairs but not downstairs.

- The structure of an igloo is so well insulated that it is possible to sit inside without a coat, while the outside temperature is as low as −40°F (−40°C).

SCIENCE AND NATURE

- The saguaro cactus requires 30 years to grow just one branch.

- The weight of air in a milk glass is about the same as the weight of one aspirin tablet.

- In many countries, urine was used as a detergent for washing. One of urine's major components, ammonia, is used in cleaning products.

- One ounce (around 28 g) of gold can be drawn to 43 miles (69 km).

- Ninety-nine per cent of all life forms that have existed on earth are now extinct.

- More than 1,500 new species have been discovered in Australian waters in the past 10 years.

- In a moderate-size office with room for 25 employees, the air can weigh nearly as much as the staff.

- The world consumes 1 billion gallons (4,546,000,000 litres) of petroleum a day.

9

RELIGION AND MYTH

RELIGION AND MYTH

- Roman Emperor Nero sentenced St Peter to crucifixion.

- The Church of the Holy Sepulchre marks the spot where Joseph of Arimathea buried Jesus.

- In the Black Forest area in Germany, religious families lay an extra place at the Christmas table for the Virgin Mary.

- Jesus gave St Peter his name. It means 'the rock'.

- The carol 'Good King Wenceslas' commemorates the martyr who is patron saint of Bohemia.

- The name 'Beelzebub' means 'lord of the flies'.

- St Jude is the patron saint of hopeless causes.

- New Zealand has had women priests since the 1960s.

- The ancient Norse associated mistletoe with their goddess of love, leading to the tradition of kissing under the mistletoe.

- In Italy, they do not use Christmas trees; instead they decorate small, pyramid-shaped wooden stands with fruit.

RELIGION AND MYTH

- In Islamic myth, Israfil is the angel who will sound the trumpet announcing the end of the world.

- It is forbidden to take photographs at a Quaker wedding.

- Orthodox Judaism forbids the practice of cremation.

- In Armenia, the traditional Christmas Eve meal consists of fried fish, lettuce and spinach.

- The longest name in the Bible is Mahershalalbaz.

- The Lord's Prayer appears twice in the Bible – in Matthew VI and Luke XI.

- Studies of the Dead Sea scrolls indicate that the passage in the Bible known as the Sermon on the Mount is actually an ancient Essene prayer dating to hundreds of years before the birth of Christ.

- Two chapters in the Bible, 2 Kings and Isaiah 37, are alike almost word for word.

- A kelpie was a water spirit of Scottish folklore, reputed to cause drownings.

- A Hindi bride wears a red sari.

─────────── **RELIGION AND MYTH** ───────────

- Christendom did not begin to date its history from the birth of Christ until 500 years after his death. The system was introduced in 550 by Dionysius Exigus, a monk in Rome.

- The 27 books of the Bible's New Testament are believed to have been written circa AD 100, about 70 to 90 years after the death of Jesus.

- A survey disclosed that 12% of Americans believe that Joan of Arc was Noah's wife.

- Portions of the Bible have been printed in 2,212 languages. A complete Bible exists in 366 languages; an additional 928 languages have a New Testament; and 918 have at least one book of the Bible.

- More than 95% of the population of Greece belongs to the Greek Orthodox Church.

- Studies show that Protestants and Jews married to Catholics have sex more frequently than those married to members of their own faith, or those in intermarriages of Protestants and Jews.

- The Roman Catholic population of the world is larger than that of all other Christian sects combined.

———————RELIGION AND MYTH ———————

- There are many patron saints for human physical
  afflictions, including St Teresa of Avila and St Denis,
  Bishop of Paris, who are the patron saints of headaches;
  St. James the Greater, patron saint of rheumatoid
  sufferers; St Apollonia, patron saint of toothaches; and St
  Genevieve (Genofeva), patron saint of fevers.

- The ancient Egyptians worshipped a sky goddess called
  Nut.

10

CUSTOMS AND TRADITIONS

CUSTOMS AND TRADITIONS

- In ancient Egypt, priests plucked every hair from their bodies, including their eyebrows and eyelashes.

- In olden days, in Britain, a green wedding dress was thought to be unlucky unless the bride was Irish. The expression that a woman had a 'green gown' implied promiscuity, as the green staining of her clothing was the result of rolling about in grassy fields with a lover.

- When a man died in ancient Egypt, the females in his family would smear their heads and faces with mud, and wander through the city beating themselves and tearing off their clothes.

- In ancient Egypt, when a woman's husband was convicted of a crime, she and her children were punished as well, usually being enslaved.

- In ancient Rome, there was a superstitious custom of nailing owls over doors, with their wings outspread, to deflect storms.

- A couple living together for two years in Russia is considered married. This is called a citizen marriage.

- In Pakistan, it is rude to show the soles of your feet or point a foot when you are sitting on the floor.

—————— CUSTOMS AND TRADITIONS ——————

- In medieval times, church bells were often consecrated to ward off evil spirits. Because thunderstorms were attributed to the work of demons, the bells would be rung in an attempt to stop the storms.

- In Russia, buying carnations or roses is a prerequisite for a first date and must be given in odd numbers, as flowers given in even numbers are reserved for funerals.

- In China, it is unwise to give the gift of a clock, as to the older Chinese generation a clock is a symbol of bad luck.

- In Jordan, when a host asks a visitor to stay for dinner it is customary to refuse twice before accepting. Unless the host insists a couple of times, seconds of any dish offered should also be refused and even then accepted only with a slight air of reluctance.

- Thai women wear black only for funerals and periods of mourning.

- Polish hospitality calls for ample food being offered, and woe to the guest who declines; yet the guest who grabs food without being encouraged disgraces himself. This is referred to as the host being a '*nukac*' – 'the one who urges.'

—————— CUSTOMS AND TRADITIONS ——————

- In Russia, yellow flowers are a sign of grieving or separation.

- In Russia, women appreciate receiving cosmetics as a gift, as they are scarce in almost all Eastern European countries.

- Until the 1950s, Tibetans disposed of their dead by taking the body up a hill, hacking it into little pieces, and feeding the remains to the birds.

- In Scotland, it is believed that if someone walks any distance between two redheaded girls, it is a sign that he or she will soon be wealthy.

- In Russia, when a friend is leaving on a trip, it is common for this person and a close friend or spouse to sit in silence on the traveller's packed suitcases for a few minutes prior to him or her departing. It is believed that this moment of togetherness will cause the traveller to have a safe journey.

- Overturned shoes (soles up) are considered very bad luck and even omens of death in Greece. If you accidentally take them off and they land soles up, turn them over immediately and say '*skorda*' (garlic) and spit once or twice.

—————— CUSTOMS AND TRADITIONS ——————

- In the highlands of Chiapas, Mexico, weaving skills are treasured, and a colourful, well-made shawl worn by an unmarried woman advises potential husbands of its wearer's dexterity.

- In Japan it is considered polite to initially refuse someone's offer of help. The Japanese may also initially refuse your offer, even if they really want or need it. Traditionally, an offer is made three times.

- In the United States, Navajo culture discourages doctors from discussing end-of-life directives and negative prognoses for fear that talking about grim subjects may trigger them.

- Some restaurants in Kyoto, Japan, have a custom called '*Ichigensan okotowari*', which means that you must be introduced by someone to be welcomed. This enables the restaurant to give its warmest hospitality and services to all its customers. Business cards are preferred to credit cards – most establishments will only accept cash.

- It is a common practice in China for people to spit or blow their noses (without a handkerchief) on a street or sidewalk. This is not considered rude, whereas blowing one's nose in a handkerchief and returning it to one's pocket is considered vulgar.

CUSTOMS AND TRADITIONS

- A hot cross bun kept from one Good Friday to the next was considered a lucky charm; it was not supposed to grow mouldy and was used as a charm against shipwreck. Good Friday bread, when hung over the chimney piece, was supposed to guarantee that all bread baked after that would be perfect.

- In Zambia, handshaking with the left hand supporting the right is common, while direct eye contact with members of the opposite sex avoided, as it may suggest romantic overtures.

- In South America, it would be rude not to ask a man about his wife and children. In most Arab countries, it would be rude to do so.

- Ancient Romans respected land boundary laws to such an extent that farmers who moved boundary stones, even if by accident, were executed, and then the guilty party's oxen were sacrificed to Jove.

- The 'fingers circle' gesture is the British sign for 'ok', but in Brazil and Germany, the gesture is considered vulgar or obscene. The gesture is also considered impolite in Greece and Russia, while in Japan it means 'money'. In Southern France, the fingers-circle sign signifies 'worthless' or 'zero'.

——— CUSTOMS AND TRADITIONS ———

- In Sweden, when leaving someone's home, the coat must not be put on until at the doorway, as to do so earlier suggests an eagerness to leave. When entering or departing a Russian home, it is considered very bad form to shake hands across the threshold.

- In Tibet, it's good manners to stick out your tongue at your guests.

- In Western culture spitting is rude, but it is common as a Russian gesture to ward off bad luck or to express the hope for continued good fortune. A Russian individual will spit three times over his or her left shoulder.

- In Thailand, the left hand is considered unclean, so should not be used when eating. Also, pointing with one finger is considered rude and is only done when pointing to objects or animals, never humans.

- The colour preference for clothes of mourning in India is brown, which symbolises withered leaves.

- When members of the Western African Wodaabe tribe greet each other, they may not look each other directly in the eyes. Also, during daylight hours, a man cannot hold his wife's hand in public, call her by name, or speak to her in a personal way.

CUSTOMS AND TRADITIONS

- The Japanese have many rules for the correct use of chopsticks. Improper use includes wandering the chopsticks over several foods without decision ('*mayoibashi*') and licking the ends of chopsticks ('*neburibashi*'), which is considered unforgivable. Similarly, chopsticks must never be used to point at somebody or be left standing up out of the food.

- In Japan, almost every weekday morning, free tissues are handed to bus and rail commuters by workers of the companies who print messages and advertisements on them. This is because most public bathrooms do not have paper towels or toilet paper.

- Among the Danakil tribesmen of Ethiopia, when a male dies, his grave is marked with a stone for every man he has killed.

- In France and Belgium, snapping the fingers of both hands has a vulgar meaning.

- An old Ethiopian tradition requires the jewellery of a bride to be removed after her wedding, with its likeness then tattooed on her skin.

- In Germany, shaking hands with the other hand in a pocket is considered impolite.

CUSTOMS AND TRADITIONS

- Natives of the Turkish village of Kuskoy communicate through whistling, allowing them to communicate over distances of up to one mile (1.6 km).

- Before eating, Japanese people say '*itadakimasu*', meaning 'I receive this food', an expression of thanks to whoever worked to prepare the food in the meal.

- In Clarendon, Texas, lawyers must accept eggs, chickens or other produce, as well as money, as payment of legal fees.

- In Egypt, social engagements usually begin very late, with dinner not served until 10.30 p.m. or later. When invited to dine, it is customary to take a gift of flowers or chocolates, though the giving and receiving of gifts should be done with both hands or with the right hand – never with the left.

- In India, it is perfectly proper for men to wear pyjamas in public, as they are accepted as standard daytime wearing apparel.

- In Mali, a man will shake hands with a woman only if she offers her hand first. The handshake is often done with the left hand touching the other person's elbow as well.

─── CUSTOMS AND TRADITIONS ───

- In Greece, it is a wedding tradition to write the names of all single female friends and relatives of the bride on the sole of her shoe. After the wedding, the shoe is examined, and those whose names have worn off are said to be the next in line for marriage.

- In America, when moving to a new home, the cat should be put in through the window, not the door, so that the animal will not leave.

- A wedding custom in early Yorkshire involved a plate holding wedding cake being thrown out of the window as the bride returned to her parental home after the wedding. If the plate broke, she would enjoy a happy future with her husband; if the plate remained intact, her future was bleak.

- From earliest times, body piercings were a superstitious practice, with the holes produced thought to release demons from the body.

- It was once the custom for French brides to step on an egg before crossing the threshold of their new homes.

- Hundreds of years ago people travelling by stagecoach in Britain often sent a servant ahead to make arrangements for their arrival. The servant would give the service

CUSTOMS AND TRADITIONS

providers money 'to ensure promptness', which was shortened by initials to 'tip'. Today a tip is more of a thank-you after good service than a bribe to get good service.

● In Anglo Saxon times, brides were often kidnapped before a wedding and brawls during the service were common. For this reason a bride stood to the groom's left at a wedding so that his sword hand would be free. This also explains why the best man stands with the groom: the tribe's best warrior was there to help the groom defend the bride.

● In Japan, frogs are the symbols of good luck.

● In Japan, the dragonfly symbolises good luck, courage, and manliness. Japanese warriors customarily wore the dragonfly emblem in battle.

● During the Middle Ages a dinner party consisting of 13 people was the worst of omens, as it foretold of the impending death of one in the group. This was associated with the Last Supper, and also with a witch's coven, as both had 13 members.

● An old folk custom for selecting a husband from several suitors involved taking onions and writing each suitor's

CUSTOMS AND TRADITIONS

name individually on each. Then all the onions were put in a cool, dark storeroom, with the first onion to grow sprouts determining which man the undecided maiden should marry.

- For a time, it was the custom to use eggs as a form of currency in France. Once a year, poverty-stricken clerics and students trudged through the streets of Paris, carrying an egg basket, and collected what they could.

- A hundred years ago, it was the custom of sailors to put a tattoo of a pig on one foot and a rooster on the other, to prevent drowning.

- Bad weather on the way to the wedding is thought to be an omen of an unhappy marriage; some cultures, however, consider rain a good omen. Cloudy skies and wind are believed to cause stormy marriages, while snow is associated with fertility and wealth.

- In Britain, a horseshoe was thought to be a guardian against all evil forces, as inhabitants of the spirit world were supposed to flee from the sight of cold iron.

- To see how many children a newlywed couple will have, the Finns count the number of grains of rice in the bride's hair. Czechs send off the newlyweds under a

────── **CUSTOMS AND TRADITIONS** ──────

barrage of peas. Italians throw sugared almonds. An African tradition is to throw corn kernels to signify fertility.

- In central Australia, it was once the custom for balding Aranda Aborigines to wear wigs made of emu feathers.

- According to old farmers' traditions, to test your love, you and your lover should each place an acorn in water. If they swim together, your love is true; if they drift apart, so will you.

- Kissing one's fingertips is a common gesture throughout Europe and Latin America countries, declaring 'Ah, beautiful!'. The gesture originates from the ancient Greeks and Romans who, when entering and leaving the temple, threw a kiss towards sacred objects such as statues and altars.

- During ancient times, egg-shaped stones were placed at the corners of a field, or by a fruit tree, to ensure a good crop. Symbolically, anything egg-shaped represented fertility.

- In 1829, New England rum was considered to be excellent for washing hair and keeping it healthy, while brandy was supposed to strengthen the roots.

CUSTOMS AND TRADITIONS

- In Iceland, tipping at a restaurant is considered an insult.

- A conventional sign of virginity in Tudor England was a high exposed bosom and a sleeve full to the wrists.

- In Britain, witches were once said to disguise themselves as cats, so many people refused to talk near a cat for fear that a witch would learn their secrets.

- According to old farmers' traditions, the best time of the day to select a new pair of shoes is in the afternoon, when the exercise of the day has stretched the muscles to their largest extent.

- Kettledrums were once used as currency on the island of Aler in Indonesia.

- Ladies in Europe took to wearing lightning rods on their hats and trailing a ground wire – a fad that began after Benjamin Franklin published instructions on how to make them, in his almanac.

- In Greek legend, malicious creatures called *kallikantzaroi* sometimes play troublesome pranks at Christmas time. To get rid of them, you would burn either salt or an old shoe, as the stench would drive them off. Other effective methods included hanging a pig's jawbone by the door

———— CUSTOMS AND TRADITIONS ————

and keeping a large fire so they couldn't sneak down the chimney.

- The widespread superstition that green is an unlucky colour dates from a centuries-old tradition that only fairies living at the bottom of the garden had the right to wear green, and would deal harshly with anyone else found wearing the colour.

- Until the 19th century, solid blocks of tea were used as money in Siberia.

- Ancient Greeks considered the philtrum, the indentation in the middle area between the nose and the upper lip, to be one of the body's most erogenous zones.

- In Victorian London, the Lord Mayor's Show always finished with a banquet that began with turtle soup.

- Iridescent beetle shells were the source of the earliest eye glitter ever used – devised by the ancient Egyptians.

- In ancient Rome, wealthy Romans always drank from goblets made of quartz crystal, as they believed the transparent mineral was a safeguard against their enemies. Legend had it that a cup carved from the transparent mineral would not hold poison.

──────── CUSTOMS AND TRADITIONS ────────

- The San Blas Indian women of Panama consider giant noses a mark of great beauty, so they paint black lines down the centre of their noses to make them appear longer.

- It was once the custom to use pieces of bread to erase lead pencil before rubber erasers came into use.

- Leather money was used in Russia up until the 17th century, as was tea money in China.

- Turkana tribesmen, who live on the barren soils of the Great Rift Valley in Kenya, add iron to their diet by drinking cows' blood – they puncture a cow's jugular vein with a sharp arrow and catch the spurting liquid in a clay jug. The cows, though bled frequently, suffer no ill effects.

- Until the 1920s, babies in Finland were often delivered in saunas. The heat was thought to help combat infection, and the warm atmosphere was considered pleasing to the infant. The Finns also considered a sauna to be a holy place.

- In America, a tip at a family restaurant should be 15% of the bill without tax, while a 10% tip is sufficient for a buffet, but you should never leave less than a quarter, even if you only have a cup of coffee.

- In Japan, white is associated with death.

11

LAWS OLD, NEW AND WEIRD

——— LAWS OLD, NEW AND WEIRD ———

- In Bahrain, a male doctor may legally examine a woman's genitals, but is prohibited from looking directly at them. He may only see their reflection in a mirror.

- Muslims are banned from looking at the genitals of a corpse. This also applies to undertakers; the organs of the deceased must be covered with a piece of wood or brick at all times.

- The penalty for masturbation in Indonesia is decapitation.

- In Hong Kong a betrayed wife is legally allowed to kill her adulterous husband, but may only do so with her bare hands. The husband's lover may be killed in any manner desired.

- Topless saleswomen are legal in Liverpool, England – but only in tropical fish stores.

- In Cali, Colombia, a woman may only have sex with her husband, and the first time this happens her mother must be in the room to witness the act.

- In New Hampshire, you may not tap your feet, nod your head, or in any way keep time to the music in a tavern, restaurant, or cafe.

LAWS OLD, NEW AND WEIRD

- In Santa Cruz, Bolivia, it is illegal for a man to have sex with a woman and her daughter at the same time.

- In Maryland, it is illegal to sell condoms from vending machines, with one exception: condoms may be dispensed from a vending machine only in places where alcoholic beverages are sold for consumption on the premises.

- In Maine, you will be charged a fine if you still have your Christmas decorations up after 14 January.

- It is illegal to 'annoy a bird' in any city park of Honolulu, Hawaii.

- In Massachusetts, taxi drivers are prohibited from making love in the front seat of their taxi during their shifts.

- In Hawaii, all residents may be fined as a result of not owning a boat.

- In Arizona, you may not have more than two dildos in a house.

- In Florida, you are not allowed to break more than three dishes per day, or chip the edges of more than four cups and/or saucers.

LAWS OLD, NEW AND WEIRD

- In Kentucky, all bees entering Kentucky shall be accompanied by certificates of health, stating that the apiary from which the bees came was free from contagious or infectious disease.

- In Iowa, kisses may last for no more than five minutes.

- In Michigan, there is a 10% bounty for each rat's head brought into a town office.

- In New Jersey, you cannot pump your own gas. All gas stations are full service, and full service only.

- In Arizona, when being attacked by a criminal or burglar, you may only protect yourself with the same weapon that the other person possesses.

- In Louisiana, biting someone with your natural teeth is 'simple assault', while biting someone with your false teeth is 'aggravated assault'.

- In Alaska, while it is legal to shoot bears, waking a sleeping bear for the purpose of taking a photograph is prohibited.

- In Fort Madison, Iowa, the fire department is required to practise fire fighting for 15 minutes before attending a fire.

LAWS OLD, NEW AND WEIRD

- In Connecticut, no one may use a white cane unless they are blind.

- In Californian animal shelters, lizards and snakes are treated under the same guidelines as cats and dogs.

- In Arizona, there is a possible 25 years prison sentence for cutting down a cactus.

- In Nebraska, if a child burps during church, his parents may be arrested.

- In Indiana, you are not allowed to carry a cocktail from the bar to a table. The waiter or waitress has to do it.

- In New Jersey, all motorists must honk before passing another car, cyclist, skater, and even a skateboarder.

- In New Jersey, it is illegal to wear a bullet-proof vest while committing a murder.

- In Massachusetts, no gorilla is allowed in the back seat of any car.

- In New York, while riding in an elevator you must talk to no one, and fold your hands while looking towards the door.

————LAWS OLD, NEW AND WEIRD————

- In Denmark, if a horse carriage is trying to pass a car and the horse becomes uneasy, the car is required to pull over and stop. If necessary, to calm the horse down, you are required to cover the car up.

- In Massachusetts, snoring is prohibited unless all bedroom windows are closed and securely locked.

- In Florida, women can be fined for falling asleep under a hair dryer, as can salon owners.

- In Indiana, you may not back into a parking spot because it prevents police officers from seeing the licence plate.

- In Massachusetts, it is illegal to go to bed without first having a full bath.

- In New Mexico, state officials ordered 400 words of 'sexually explicit material' to be cut from *Romeo and Juliet.*

- In Nevada, it is still 'legal' to hang someone for shooting your dog on your property.

- In Montana, it is illegal for married women to go fishing alone on Sundays, and illegal for unmarried women to fish alone at all.

LAWS OLD, NEW AND WEIRD

- In Massachusetts, it is unlawful to injure a football goal post. Doing so is punishable by a $200 fine.

- In Louisiana, it is illegal to gargle in public places.

- In Alabama, it is illegal for a driver to be blindfolded while operating a vehicle.

- In Indiana, baths may not be taken between the months of October and March.

- In Alabama, bogies may not be flicked into the wind.

- In Alabama, it is illegal to impersonate any type of minister, of any religion.

- In Alabama, putting salt on a rail-road track may be punishable by death.

- In Indiana, no one may catch a fish with their bare hands.

- In Georgia, it is illegal to use profanity in front of a dead body lying in a funeral home or in a coroner's office.

- In Kentucky, it is illegal to fish with a bow and arrow.

- In Arizona, it is unlawful to refuse a person a glass of water.

——— LAWS OLD, NEW AND WEIRD ———

- In New York, a fine of $25 can be levied for flirting. This old law specifically prohibits men from turning round on any city street and looking 'at a woman in that way'. A second conviction for a crime of this magnitude calls for the violating male to be forced to wear a 'pair of horse-blinders', wherever and whenever he goes outside for a stroll.

- In Kansas, pedestrians crossing the highways at night must wear tail-lights.

- In Massachusetts, bullets may not be used as currency.

- In Connecticut, in order for a pickle to officially be considered a pickle, it must bounce.

- In Florida, if an elephant is left tied to a parking meter, the parking fee has to be paid just as it would for a vehicle.

- In Massachusetts, it is illegal to allow someone to use stilts while working on the construction of a building.

- In Florida, it is illegal to skateboard without a licence.

- In Alabama, it is illegal to wear a fake moustache that causes laughter in church.

LAWS OLD, NEW AND WEIRD

- In Colorado, car dealers may not show cars on a Sunday.

- In New Jersey, it is against the law to 'frown' at a police officer.

- In Indiana, it is illegal for a liquor store to sell cold soft drinks.

- In Minnesota, citizens may not enter Wisconsin with a chicken on their head.

- In Montana, it is a misdemeanour to show movies that depict acts of felonious crime.

- In Kansas, if two trains meet on the same track, neither shall proceed until the other has passed.

- In Georgia, signs are required to be written in English.

- In Indiana, if any person has a puppet show, wire dancing or tumbling act in the state of Indiana and receives money for it, they will be fined $3 under the Act to Prevent Certain Immoral Practices.

- In California, animals are banned from mating publicly within 1,500 ft (457 m) of a bar, school, or place of worship.

───── LAWS OLD, NEW AND WEIRD ─────

- In Michigan, it is legal for a robber to file a lawsuit, if he or she got hurt in your house.

- In Indiana, a $3 fine per pack will be imposed on anyone playing cards, under the Act for the Prevention of Gaming.

- In Illinois, you may be convicted of a Class 4 felony offence, punishable by up to three years in state prison, for the crime of 'eavesdropping' on your own conversation.

- In Louisiana, it is illegal to rob a bank and then shoot at the bank teller with a water pistol.

- In Nebraska, it is illegal for a mother to give her daughter a perm without a state licence.

- In Indiana, a man over the age of 18 may be arrested for statutory rape if the passenger in his car is not wearing her socks and shoes, and is under the age of 17.

- In Fairbanks, Alaska, it is illegal to feed alcoholic beverages to a moose.

- In Michigan, any person over the age of 12 may have a licence for a hand-gun as long as he or she has not been convicted of a felony.

LAWS OLD, NEW AND WEIRD

- In Iowa, a man with a moustache may never kiss a woman in public.

- In Arizona, any misdemeanour committed while wearing a red mask is considered a felony. This goes back to the days of the Wild West.

- In Georgia, you have the right to commit simple battery if provoked by 'fighting' words.

- In Indiana, anyone the age of 14 or older who profanely curses, damns or swears by the name of God, Jesus Christ or the Holy Ghost, shall be fined between $1 and $3 for each offence, with a maximum fine of $10 per day.

- In Idaho, you may not fish on a camel's back.

- In Massachusetts, affiliation with the Communist Party is illegal.

- In Montana, it is illegal to have a sheep in the cab of your truck without a chaperone.

- In Kentucky, it is illegal to fish in the Ohio River in Kentucky without an Indiana Fishing Licence.

- In Florida, it is illegal to block any travelled wagon road.

———— LAWS OLD, NEW AND WEIRD ————

- In New York, a person may not walk around on Sundays with an ice-cream cone in his or her pocket.

- In Michigan, a woman isn't allowed to cut her own hair without her husband's permission.

- In Massachusetts, tomatoes may not be used in the production of clam chowder.

- In Connecticut, you can be stopped by the police for cyling over 65 mph (105 kph).

- In New York, it is against the law to throw a ball at someone's head for fun.

- In California, it is a misdemeanour to shoot at any kind of game from a moving vehicle, unless the target is a whale.

- In Indiana, drinks on the house are illegal.

- In Ireland, wearing a Halloween costume could result in up to one year in prison.

- In Georgia, members of the state assembly cannot be ticketed for speeding while the state assembly is in session.

—LAWS OLD, NEW AND WEIRD—

- In Alaska, moose may not be viewed from a plane.

- In Indiana, hotel sheets must be exactly 99 inches (251 cm) long and 81 inches (206 cm) wide.

- In Nebraska, it is illegal to go whale fishing.

- In New Jersey, you may not slurp your soup.

- In Massachusetts, public boxing matches are outlawed.

- In Arizona, donkeys cannot sleep in bathtubs.

- In Maine, shotguns are required to be taken to church in the event of a Native American attack.

- In Nevada, it is illegal to drive a camel on the highway.

- In New Hampshire, you cannot sell the clothes you are wearing to pay off a gambling debt.

- In Iowa, one-armed piano players must perform free of charge.

- In Spearfish, South Dakota, if three or more American Indians are walking down the street together, they can be considered a war party and fired upon.

LAWS OLD, NEW AND WEIRD

- In Arkansas, alligators may not be kept in bathtubs.

- In New York, a licence must be purchased before hanging clothes on a clothes-line.

- In Mississippi, horses are not to be housed within 50 ft (15 m) of any road.

- In Florida, penalty for horse theft is death by hanging.

- In Indiana, moustaches are illegal if the bearer has a tendency to habitually kiss other humans.

- In Maine, you may not step out of a plane in flight.

- In South Carolina, merchandise may not be sold within a half mile (0.8 km) of a church, unless fruit is being sold.

- In Massachusetts, it is illegal to drive Texan, Mexican, Cherokee or other American Indian cattle on a public road.

- In Alabama, incestuous marriages are legal.

- In Montana, it is a felony for a wife to open her husband's mail.

LAWS OLD, NEW AND WEIRD

- In Montana, seven or more American Indians are considered a raiding or war party, and it is legal to shoot them.

- In Idaho, riding a merry-go-round on Sundays is considered a crime.

- In Colorado, it is illegal to ride a horse while under the influence.

- In Massachusetts, mourners may eat no more than three sandwiches during a wake.

- In California, sunshine is guaranteed to the masses.

- In Hawaii, coins are not allowed to be placed in a person's ears.

- In New Hampshire, it is illegal to pick up seaweed off the beach.

- In Minnesota, all men driving motorcycles must wear shirts.

- In 17th-century Japan, no citizen was allowed to leave the country on penalty of death. Anyone caught coming or going without permission was executed on the spot.

LAWS OLD, NEW AND WEIRD

- In Minnesota, all bathtubs must have feet.

- In Indiana, smoking in the state legislature building is banned, except when the legislature is in session.

- In New Jersey, spray paint may not be sold without a posted sign warning juveniles of the penalty for creating graffiti.

- Jaguar images and costumes were outlawed by the Catholic Church in the 17th century because of their association with Indian religion, militia and politics.

- In Alabama, dominoes may not be played on Sunday.

- In Iowa, it is illegal to sell or distribute drugs or narcotics without having first obtained the appropriate Iowa drug tax stamp.

- In Florida, having sexual relations with a porcupine is illegal.

- It is against the law for a monster to enter the corporate limits of Urbana, Illinois.

- In Norway, you may not spay your female dog or cat. However, you may neuter the males of the species.

————LAWS OLD, NEW AND WEIRD ————

- The minimum age for marriage of Italian girls was raised by law to 12 years in 1892.

- In 17th-century Massachusetts, smoking was legal only at a distance of five miles (8 km) from any town.

- In ancient Cambodia, it was illegal to insult a rice plant.

- In 1845, Boston banned bathing unless you had a doctor's prescription.

- In the 1630s, a decree in Japan forbade the building of any large ocean-worthy ships, to deter defection.

- It was illegal for women to wear buttons in 15th-century Florence.

- During the 15th century, the handkerchief was for a time allowed only to the nobility, with special laws made to enforce this.

- In Canada, if a debt is higher than 25 cents, it is illegal to pay it with pennies.

- In the latter part of the 1300s, dress code laws in Florence, Italy, stipulated precisely the depth of a woman's *décolletage*.

LAWS OLD, NEW AND WEIRD

- In Florida it is illegal to release more than ten lighter-than-air balloons at a time. This is to protect marine creatures that often mistake balloons for food and can suffer intestinal injuries if they eat the balloons.

- In Massachusetts, it is illegal to keep a mule on the second floor of a building not in a city, unless there are two exits.

- It is unlawful to lend your vacuum cleaner to your next-door neighbour in Denver, Colorado.

- The Germans considered *Casablanca* (1942) a propaganda film and made it illegal to show in German theatres during World War II. Even after the war, only a censored version was allowed to be shown in Germany, with all references to Nazis removed.

- On Sundays, in New Hampshire, citizens may not relieve themselves while looking up.

- It is illegal to drink beer out of a bucket while you're sitting on a kerb in St Louis, Missouri.

- In London, you will face a 24-hour detainment if you are caught sticking gum under a seat on the upper deck of a bus.

LAWS OLD, NEW AND WEIRD

- In Natoma, Kansas, it's illegal to throw knives at men wearing striped suits.

- In Florida it is illegal to litter intentionally with plastic fishing gear or lines.

- A law in Illinois prohibits barbers from using their fingers to apply shaving cream to a patron's face.

- In Atwoodville, Connecticut, it is illegal to play Scrabble while waiting for a politician to speak.

- Connecticut and Rhode Island never ratified the 18th Amendment: Prohibition.

- It is against the law to pawn your dentures in Las Vegas.

- Twenty-two inches (56 cm) is the minimum legal length for commercial sale of California halibut.

- The penalty for conviction of smuggling in Bangladesh is the death penalty.

- During the fourth century in Sparta, Greece, if you were male and over 20 years of age, you were required by law to eat 2 lb (0.9 kg) of meat a day, as it was supposed to make a person brave.

LAWS OLD, NEW AND WEIRD

- The sale of chewing gum is outlawed in Singapore because it is a means of 'tainting an environment free of dirt'.

- In Germany and Argentina, a screwing gesture at your head, meaning 'You're crazy', is illegal when driving.

- No store is allowed to sell a toothbrush on the Sabbath in Providence, Rhode Island. Yet these same stores are allowed to sell toothpaste and mouthwash on Sundays.

- Candy made from pieces of barrel cactus is illegal in the United States, to protect the species.

- Dancing to the 'Star-Spangled Banner' is against the law in several American states.

- In Kentucky, it is against the law to throw eggs at a public speaker.

- In London, it is illegal to drive a car without sitting in the front seat.

- No two-cycle engines are allowed in Singapore. The licence fee for a new car is small, about £2.50, but as the vehicle grows older, the fee increases. When the car reaches eight years old, it is no longer allowed on the

—LAWS OLD, NEW AND WEIRD—

streets. These strict laws have virtually wiped out air pollution in the country.

- The state of Vera Cruz, in Mexico, outlaws priests as citizens.

- In colonial America, tobacco was acceptable legal tender in several southern colonies, and in Virginia, taxes were paid in tobacco.

- For hundreds of years, the Chinese zealously guarded the secret of sericulture; imperial law decreed death by torture to those who disclosed how to make silk.

- In Milan, Italy, there is a law that requires a smile on the face of all citizens at all times. Exemptions include time spent visiting patients in hospitals or attending funerals. Otherwise, a person may be fined £55 if they are seen in public without a smile on their face.

- No patent can ever be taken out on a gambling machine in the United States.

- In St Catalina, unlike the rest of Southern California, the number of cars on the island is strictly limited. The waiting time for a car permit is eight to ten years, so most residents drive electric-powered golf carts.

LAWS OLD, NEW AND WEIRD

- Under Norwegian law, a polar bear may be shot only if deemed a menace.

- Oxford University requires all members upon admission to the Bodleian Library to read aloud a pledge that includes an agreement to not 'kindle therein any fire or flame'. Regulations also prohibit readers bringing sheep into the library.

- In New Mexico, it is against the law to ship horned toads out of the state.

- In New York State, it is illegal to shoot a rabbit from a moving trolley car.

- In North Dakota, it is legal to shoot an American Indian on horseback, provided you are in a covered wagon.

- Texas is the only state that permits residents to cast absentee ballots from space. The first to exercise this right to vote while in orbit was astronaut David Wolf, who cast his vote for Houston mayor via e-mail from the Russian space station *Mir* in November 1997.

- Pennsylvania law mandates that each year all counties provide veterans' graves with flags, most of which are distributed before Memorial Day.

——————LAWS OLD, NEW AND WEIRD ——————

- In Pacific Grove, California, it is a misdemeanour to kill a butterfly.

- The states of Vermont, Alaska, Hawaii and Maine do not allow billboards.

- In Pennsylvania, ministers are forbidden from performing marriages when either the bride or groom is drunk.

- Until about 150 years ago, church-going was required by law in Britain.

- In Riverside, California, it is illegal to kiss, unless both people wipe their lips with rose-water.

- In San Salvador, El Salvador, drunk drivers can be punished by death before a firing squad.

- In Sandusky, Ohio, anyone older than age 14 looking for goodies at Halloween is breaking the law.

- Scandinavian law forbids television advertising of foods to children.

- Officials of ancient Greece decreed that mollusc shells be used as ballots, because once a vote was scratched on the shell, it couldn't be erased or altered.

LAWS OLD, NEW AND WEIRD

- In some smaller towns in the state of Arizona, it is illegal to wear suspenders.

- Christmas carolling is banned at two major malls in Pensacola, Florida, as shoppers and shopkeepers complained that the carollers were too loud and took up too much space.

- In Somalia, it has been decreed illegal to carry old chewing gum stuck on the tip of your nose.

- In Arizona, a hunting licence is required by law to hunt rattlesnakes, but not to own them as pets.

- Women are banned by royal decree from using hotel swimming pools in Jidda, Saudi Arabia.

- There is a law in South Pittsburg, Tennessee, also known as 'The Cornbread Capitol of the World', concerning the cooking of this southern staple. The law declares: 'Cornbread isn't cornbread unless it be made correctly. Therefore, all cornbread must be hereby made in nothing other then a cast-iron skillet. Those found in violation of this ordinance are to be fined one dollar.'

- It is illegal to marry the spouse of a grandparent in Maine, Maryland, South Carolina and Washington DC.

─────LAWS OLD, NEW AND WEIRD ─────

- In Winnetka, Illinois, while you are in a theatre it is against the law to remove your shoes if your feet smell bad.

- In the United States, federal law states that children's TV shows may contain only 10 minutes of advertising per hour, and on weekends the limit is 10 1/2 minutes.

- In the state of Queensland, Australia, it is still constitutional law that all pubs must have a railing outside for patrons to tie up their horse.

- In Hazelton, Pennsylvania, it is illegal to sip a carbonated drink while lecturing students in a school auditorium.

- It is against the law to yell out 'Snake!' within the city limits of Flowery Branch, Georgia.

- In New York City it is illegal to make your living through the skinning of horses or cows, the growing of ragweed, or the burning of bones.

- Until 1893, lynching was legal in the United States. The first anti-lynching law was passed in Georgia, but it only made the violation punishable by four years in prison.

- In Britain, the law was changed in 1789 to make hanging the method of execution, instead of burning.

———— LAWS OLD, NEW AND WEIRD ————

- When John F Kennedy was assassinated, it was not illegal to kill the president of the United States.

- Licensed London taxis are required by law to carry a bale of hay at all times, dating from the days of the horse-drawn cab. The relevant law has never been revoked.

- The Kentucky Supreme Court has ruled that the prosecution must throw its files wide open to the defence if the accused is suffering from amnesia.

- In 1547, British law was amended to end the practice of boiling people to death as punishment for criminal behaviour.

- In the US, in 1832, a law was passed requiring all American citizens to spend one day each year fasting and praying. People ignored the law, and no effort was made to enforce the legislation.

- The US Supreme Court once ruled federal income tax unconstitutional. It was first imposed during the Civil War as a temporary revenue-raising measure.

- In 1908, a law was passed in New York City making it illegal for women to smoke in public.

---LAWS OLD, NEW AND WEIRD---

- In Greenwich, UK, during the 1800s it was unlawful to impersonate a retired person on a pension.

- LSD was legal in California until 1967.

- According to US law, a patent may not be granted on a useless invention or on a machine that will not operate. Even if an invention is novel or new, a patent may not be obtained if the invention would have been obvious to a person having ordinary skill in the same area at the time of the invention.

- In 1984, the Minnesota State Legislature ordered that all gender-specific language, which referred only to one gender, usually men, be removed from the state laws. After two years of work, the rewritten laws were adopted. The word 'his' was changed 10,000 times and 'he' was changed 6,000 times.

- It was only after John F Kennedy was assassinated that Congress enacted a law making it a federal crime to kill, kidnap, or assault the president, vice-president or president-elect.

- It was only in 1968 that the state of Tennessee abolished its anti-evolution law and accepted the doctrine of evolution.

—— LAWS OLD, NEW AND WEIRD ——

● Murdering a travelling musician was not a serious crime in Britain during the Middle Ages.

● Private cars were forbidden on the island of Bermuda until 1948, explaining why there are still so many bicycles there.

● Married women were forbidden by law to watch, let alone compete, in the ancient Olympics, the penalty being death. The Greeks believed that the presence of wives in Olympia would defile Greece's oldest religious shrine there, although young girls were allowed in. Women who broke the rule were thrown from a nearby cliff.

● In Gwinnett County, Georgia, it is illegal for residents to keep rabbits as pets, with rabbits restricted to farm areas and homes with at least three acres (1.2 hectares) of land. However, the law was amended in 1993 to allow Vietnamese pot-bellied pigs as pets after a woman with a pet pig pleaded for the exemption.

● The design of a US coin cannot be changed more than once in 25 years without special legislation by Congress.

● During World War II, US ice-cream manufacturers were restricted by law to produce only 20 different flavours of ice-cream.

LAWS OLD, NEW AND WEIRD

- E-signatures have the same legal standing as handwritten signatures.

- The first state minimum wage law in the United States went into effect in Massachusetts in 1913. It would be another 25 years before the minimum wage law went into effect, nationally providing a minimum wage of 25 cents an hour.

- In December 1997, the state of Nevada became the first state to pass legislation categorising Y2K data disasters as 'acts of God' – protecting the state from lawsuits that may potentially be brought against it by residents in the year 2000.

- In Scotland, all people of nobility are free from all arrests for debts, as they are the king's hereditary counsellors. They cannot be outlawed in any civil action, and no attachment lies against their persons.

- In Britain, a Witchcraft Act of the early 1700s identified black cats as dangerous animals to be shunned.

- Circus showman P T Barnum created a spectacle when he hitched an elephant to a plough beside the train tracks to announce that his circus had come to town. As a result, Barnum attracted many newsmen and the

——— LAWS OLD, NEW AND WEIRD ———

public, but thereafter it soon became illegal in North
Carolina to plough a field with an elephant. The law still
remains to this day.

- In Britain, in 1571, a man could be fined for not
wearing a wool cap.

- In France, Napoleon instituted a scale of fines for sex
offences, which included 35 francs for a man guilty of
lifting a woman's skirt to the knee and 70 francs if he
lifted it to the thigh.

- In the 1940s, California law made it illegal to serve
alcohol to a homosexual or someone dressed as a
member of the opposite sex. Drag queens avoided the
latter restriction by attaching pieces of paper to their
dresses that read 'I'm a boy'. The courts accepted the
argument that anyone wearing such a notice was
technically dressed as a man, not a woman.

- During the Renaissance period, laws were passed that
prescribed which fashions could not be worn by the
lower classes, so as to keep social distinctions intact.
Queen Elizabeth I of England would not allow the ruff
to be worn by commoners; in Florence, women of the
lower class were not allowed to use buttons of certain
shapes and materials.

LAWS OLD, NEW AND WEIRD

- During the reign of Catherine I of Russia, the rules for parties stipulated that no man was to get drunk before 9 o'clock, and ladies were not to get drunk at any hour.

- It was against the law to tie a male horse next to a female horse on Main Street in Wetaskiwin, Canada, in 1917.

- Centuries ago, in London, someone drinking at a tavern had the legal right to demand to see the wine cellar to verify that the wine hadn't been watered down. Refusal by the taverner could result in severe penalties, including time in prison.

- The California Board of Equalization has ruled that bartenders cannot be held responsible for misjudging the age of midgets.

- Barbie dolls are considered anti-Islamic and importing them to Iran is prohibited. However, in the late 1990s dozens of shops in Tehran displayed original all-American Barbie dolls, some wearing only a swimsuit. A 3-ft-tall (0.9 m) Barbie bride model was selling for as much as £390 in a country where the average monthly salary was £55.

- Due to heavy traffic congestion, Julius Caesar banned all wheeled vehicles from Rome during daylight hours.

——— LAWS OLD, NEW AND WEIRD ———

- The Recruitment Code of the US Navy states that anyone 'bearing an obscene and indecent' tattoo will be rejected.

- Before 1933, the dime was legal as payment only in transactions of $10 or less. In that year, Congress made the dime legal tender for all transactions.

- The US Government will not allow portraits of living persons to appear on stamps.

12

SPORTS AND GAMES

SPORTS AND GAMES

- Between two and three jockeys are killed each year in horse-racing.

- Horse-racing regulations state that no racehorse's name may contain more than 18 letters. Names that are too long would be cumbersome on racing sheets.

- Statistics show that at racetracks, the favourite wins less than 30% of all horse races.

- The most landed-on square in Monopoly is Trafalgar Square.

- To prevent some numbers from occurring more frequently than others, dice used in crap games in Las Vegas are manufactured to a tolerance of 0.0002 inches (0.0005 cm), less than 1/17 the thickness of a human hair.

- In 1950, at the Las Vegas Desert Inn, an anonymous sailor made 27 straight wins with the dice at craps. The odds against such a feat are 12,467,890 to 1. The dice today are enshrined in the hotel on a velvet pillow under glass.

- In Japan, the deadly martial art called 'tessenjutsu' is based solely on the use of a fan.

SPORTS AND GAMES

- The Nike 'swoosh' logo was designed by University of Oregon student Carolyn Davidson in 1964 and she was paid $35 dollars for her design.

- The game of Monopoly is the best-selling board game in the world, licensed or sold in 80 countries and produced in 26 languages.

- An estimated £600,000 is lost at racetracks each year by people who lose or carelessly throw away winning tickets.

- More cheating takes place in private, friendly gambling games than in all other gambling games combined.

- The children's game Rock, Paper, Scissors is also popular in Japan, where it is called Janken. The game is also played by some children using their feet, with closed feet equalling stone (*gu*), spread legs equalling paper (*pa*) and one foot behind the other equalling scissors (*choki*).

- There are 170,000,000,000,000,000,000,000,000,000 ways to play the 10 opening moves in a game of chess.

- Alec Brown invented a miniature snooker cue the size of a fountain pen for tricky shots, but it was outlawed because of its size in 1938.

SPORTS AND GAMES

- On a bingo card of 90 numbers, there are approximately 44 million ways to make B-I-N-G-O.

- A twice-retaken penalty kick for Notts County at Portsmouth in 1973 was missed by all three takers – Don Masson, Brian Stubbs and Kevin Randall.

- The game Scrabble is found in one out of every three American homes.

- Model soldiers date back 4,000 years to ancient Egypt.

- The highest known score for a single word in competition Scrabble is 392. In 1982, Dr Saladin Khoshnaw achieved this score for the word 'caziques', which means an Indian chief.

- Since the Lego Group began manufacturing blocks in 1949, more than 189 billion pieces in 2,000 different shapes have been produced. This is enough for about 30 Lego pieces for every living person on earth.

- The longest recorded Monopoly game was 1,680 hours – more than 70 days.

- Damon Hill worked as a motorcycle despatch rider from 1982–85.

SPORTS AND GAMES

- Full seeding at Wimbledon began in 1927.

- There was a total prize-money fund of £10 for the British Golf Open in 1863.

- US boxer Sugar Ray Leonard won titles at five different weights.

- About 50 competitors in the 1999 Dakar Rally were held up and robbed at gunpoint after the end of the 12th stage.

- Ladies used blue cricket balls during Edwardian times in case they became over-excited at the prospect of red ones.

- The sin bin was introduced in rugby league in 1983.

- From 1985–91 Boris Becker only once failed to appear in the Wimbledon men's singles final, in 1987.

- Eight competitors took part in the 1860 British Golf Open.

- The two courses at Emirates Golf Club in Dubai need two million gallons (9,092,000 litres) of water each day during the summer to keep them in condition.

——————— SPORTS AND GAMES ———————

● Charlotte Brew was the first woman to ride in the Grand National.

● Fifteen teams entered the first FA Cup competition.

● A mouse stopped play in the 1962 Edgbaston Test between England and Pakistan.

● A French infantry captain named Mingaud invented the leather tip of a snooker cue in 1807.

● FIFA referee Ken Aston thought up the idea of red and yellow cards.

● The Azteca, Etrusco, Questra and Tricolore were all types of football used for World Cup Final tournaments.

● England cricketer J W H T Douglas also won the 1908 Olympic middleweight boxing gold medal.

● The 1979/80 Bangalore Test Match between India and Pakistan was halted due to the invasion of a swarm of bees.

● Manchester United's mascot Fred the Red had his nose broken during the squad's overzealous celebration of the 1996 Premiership.

SPORTS AND GAMES

- The original FA Cup was stolen 1895 and never recovered.

- Singapore hosted a RoboCup in 1998, involving teams of robot footballers.

- Wigan rugby league club's mascot is Pie Man.

- Greg Norman caddied for his son in the Junior British Open in 1998.

- A Formula 1 tyre costs approximately £850.

- The first set of ice hockey rules were drawn up in 1865.

- The New York Met's baseball manager Bobby Valentine received a two-match ban when he attempted to retake his seat on the bench in a game against the Toronto Blue Jays after having been sent off for arguing too fiercely. He disguised himself in a cap, sunglasses and false moustache but was spotted by TV cameras.

- Sumner, Bramich and McKee are all types of hares used in greyhound racing.

- Cricketer Sachin Tendulkar scored seven Test centuries before his 21st birthday.

——————— SPORTS AND GAMES ———————

- A fan at the 1999 Phoenix Golf Open was arrested for carrying a gun.

- Only eight players have scored a total of 10 or more goals in World Cup Finals tournaments.

- A rubber cube was originally used instead of a ball in hockey.

- Sweden pioneered orienteering.

- The original basket in basketball, as invented by James Naismith in 1891, was a peach basket.

- Mark and Steve Waugh were the first twins to play Test cricket.

- Cricketer Imran Khan studied at Keble College, Oxford.

- The 1977 League Cup Final was replayed twice.

- Margaret Thatcher is Honorary Vice-President of Blackburn Rovers.

- Rocky Marciano is the only world-heavyweight-boxing champion to remain undefeated throughout his entire professional career.

SPORTS AND GAMES

- The standard size of a clay pigeon is 120 mm in diameter with a 26 mm breadth.

- British tennis rivals Tim Henman and Greg Rusedski share the same birthday.

- Escrima is a Philippine martial art using sticks, knives and hands.

- The official width of a cricket bat is 4 inches (10 cm).

- The ancient Olympic Games started in 776 BC.

- Octupush is an underwater hockey game played between teams.

- The first Grand Prix World Championship was held in 1950.

- Cricketer Denis Compton also won an FA Cup winner's medal with Arsenal.

- Olympic double-winning marathon runner Abebe Bikila won one race barefoot, the other in shoes.

- Numbers on the backs of FA Cup shirts were first in evidence in 1933.

SPORTS AND GAMES

- Amateur baseball players are called sandlotters.

- The ancient Olympic Games ended in 395 BC as Olympia was destroyed by an earthquake.

- Putting on the green is called the 'game within a game'.

- Bruce, Danforth and Meon are all types of anchor.

- Torquay United banned pre-match kickabout shots aimed at the goal, fearing legal action from fans hit by misses.

- The Boston Marathon is the world's oldest annual race, starting in 1897.

- West Ham's Paolo Futre exited Highbury before a game with Arsenal because he wasn't allowed to wear the number 10 shirt.

- When the first tennis racquets appeared in the 1920s the strings were made from piano wire.

- Cricketer Ian Botham's son Liam played county cricket for Hampshire.

- George Ligowsky invented the clay pigeon in the 1880s.

—————— SPORTS AND GAMES ——————

- British father and son Donald and Michael Campbell both held the land speed record.

- The line from behind which the darts are thrown is called the 'hockey'.

- Synchronised swimming was introduced to the Olympics in 1984.

- The US race meeting Breeders Cup Day is the richest day's sport in the world.

- The Virginia Slims tennis championship is the only tournament where women play the best of five sets.

- Yorker, googly and chinaman are styles of bowling in cricket.

- A badminton racquet was once known as a battledore.

- Two is the lowest possible score to conclude a game of darts.

- Dutch and German immigrants introduced ninepin bowling to the US.

- The horizontal lines on a chessboard are called ranks.

SPORTS AND GAMES

- The FA Cup Final was replayed in successive years from 1981–83.

- Cricketer Ian Botham also played football for Scunthorpe United.

- Snooker was invented in India.

13

THE WORLD AND ITS PEOPLE

THE WORLD AND ITS PEOPLE

- A pickled snake bit Li of Suzhou, China, when he opened a bottle of rice wine.

- As Hitler's body was never found, a German court officially declared Hitler dead as recently as 1956.

- More than 50% of the people in the world have never made or received a telephone call.

- The average human eats eight spiders at night in their lifetime.

- Smokers eat more sugar than non-smokers do.

- All the chemicals in the human body have a combined value of approximately £4

- In ancient Sparta, Greece, married men were not allowed to live with their wives until they turned 30.

- Dorothy Parker wanted 'this is on me' on her tombstone.

- Half the world's population is under 25 years of age.

- In 1994, Chicago artist Dwight Kalb sent US talk-show host David Letterman a statue of Madonna, made of 180 lb (82 kg) of ham.

THE WORLD AND ITS PEOPLE

- The people killed most often during bank robberies are the robbers.

- An exocannibal eats only enemies, while an indocannibal eats only friends.

- Howard Hughes never once attended a board of directors meeting, or any sort of meeting, at any of the companies he owned.

- King Louis XIV of France established in his court the position of 'Royal Chocolate Maker to the King'.

- Napoleon reportedly carried chocolate on all his military campaigns.

- In 1973, Swedish confectionery salesman Roland Ohlsson was buried in a coffin made entirely of chocolate.

- Someone's gender can be guessed with 95% accuracy just by smelling his or her breath.

- On average, Elizabeth Taylor has remarried every four years, five months.

- Pontius Pilate was born in Scotland.

THE WORLD AND ITS PEOPLE

- When he was young Leonardo da Vinci drew a picture of a horrible monster and placed it near a window in order to surprise his father. The drawing was so convincing that, upon seeing it, his father believed it to be real and set out to protect his family until the boy showed him it was just a picture. Da Vinci's father then enrolled his son in an art class.

- Ten per cent of *Star Trek* fans replace the lenses on their glasses every five years, whether they need to or not.

- Ancient Romans at one time used human urine as an ingredient in their toothpaste.

- People who are lying to you tend to look up and to the left.

- The middle name of Jimmy Hoffa is Riddle. The legendary American union figure disappeared without trace on 30 July 1975.

- Boys who have unusual first names are more likely to have mental problems than boys with conventional names.

- One in three consumers pays off his or her credit card bill every month.

———— THE WORLD AND ITS PEOPLE ————

- Pop star Justin Timberlake's half-eaten French toast sold for over $3,000 on eBay.

- One in three snakebite victims is drunk. One in five is tattooed.

- More than 50% of lottery players go back to work after winning the jackpot.

- Michelangelo was harshly criticised by a Vatican official for the nudity in his fresco *The Last Judgement*, which hangs on the walls of the Sistine Chapel in Rome. In retaliation the artist made some changes to his work: he painted in the face of the complaining clergyman and added donkey's ears and a snake's tail.

- Children who are breast-fed tend to have an IQ seven points higher than children who are not.

- Male hospital patients fall out of bed twice as often as female hospital patients.

- Less than 10% of criminals commit about 67% of all crime.

- We inhale about 700,000 of our own skin flakes each day.

THE WORLD AND ITS PEOPLE

- The Nestlés haven't run Nestlé since 1875.

- Astronauts get taller when they are in space.

- Although Howard Hughes had 15 personal attendants and three doctors on full-time duty, he died of neglect and malnutrition, caused by his intense desire to be left alone.

- Every queen named Jane has been murdered, imprisoned, gone mad, died young, or been dethroned.

- When a person is wide awake, alert, and mentally active, they are still only 25% aware of what various parts of their body are doing.

- It's been estimated that men have been riding horses for over 3,000 years.

- The make-up entrepreneur Elizabeth Arden's real name was Florence Nightingale Graham, but she changed it once her company became successful at the beginning of the 1900s.

- Heavyweight boxing champion George Foreman has five sons named George, George Jnr, George III, George IV, George V and George VI.

———THE WORLD AND ITS PEOPLE———

- A five-and-a-half-year-old weighing 250 lb (113 kg) was exhibited at a meeting of the Physical Society of Vienna on 4 December 1894. She ate a normal diet and was otherwise in good health but she wasn't able to sweat.

- People who have computers in their homes tend to watch 40% less television than average.

- A German soldier was riding in the back seat of a World War I plane when the engine suddenly stalled and he fell out of his seat while over two miles (3 km) above ground. As he was falling, the plane started falling too, and he was blown back into his own seat by the wind and was able to land the plane safely.

- Queen Elizabeth I named a man as the 'Official Uncorker of Bottles', and passed a law that stated all bottles found washed up on beaches had to be opened by him and no one else, in case they contained sensitive military messages. The penalty for anyone else opening a bottle was the death sentence.

- People overwhelmingly tend to marry partners who live near them.

- Afraid of growing old, Countess Bathory of Hungary became convinced that if she bathed in the blood of

──── THE WORLD AND ITS PEOPLE ────

young girls, she could stay young for ever, and so for 10 years she drained the blood of imprisoned girls so that she could take 'blood baths' in a huge iron vat. After one intended victim escaped, the King of Hungary ordered his soldiers to storm her castle. When they found many dead and some still-alive bodies, they locked the countess inside her room and bricked it up, leaving only a small opening through which she was given food until she died.

- Charles Darwin cured his snuff habit by keeping his snuffbox in the basement and the key for the snuffbox in the attic.

- Voltaire drank between 50 and 65 cups of coffee every day.

- Manfredo Settala (1600–1680) is the only person in all recorded history that has been killed by a meteorite.

- Rembrandt died penniless with a friend coming up with the £2.85 it cost to bury him.

- Young children are poisoned by houseplants more often than by detergents and other chemicals.

- An Indian emperor was given four wives when he inherited the throne at the age of eight.

--------- **THE WORLD AND ITS PEOPLE** ---------

- Riverdance star Michael Flatley is also an accomplished concert flute player, a champion boxer and a chess master. He has been listed by the National Geographic Society as a 'Living Treasure'.

- Pablo Picasso has sold more works of art individually costing over $1 million than any other artist. 211 Picasso pieces have topped the million dollar mark, well ahead of the 168 Pierre-Auguste Renoir works sold over this amount.

- When there is no one else waiting to use a public phone, callers average 90 seconds' talking, but if someone is waiting, the callers average four minutes per call.

- Men more often dream about their male heroes, bosses, friends or role models than about women.

- Howard Hughes became so compulsive about germs that he used to spend hours swabbing his arms over and over again with rubbing alcohol.

- In 1949, Jack Wurm, an unemployed man, was aimlessly walking on a California beach when he came across a washed-up bottle containing this message: 'To avoid confusion, I leave my entire estate to the lucky person who finds this bottle and to my attorney, Barry Cohen,

——— THE WORLD AND ITS PEOPLE ———

share and share alike. Daisy Alexander, June 20, 1937.' It was not a hoax and Mr Wurm received over $6 million from the Alexander estate.

- W C Fields used to open savings accounts everywhere he went. He put over £500,000 in 700 different banks but couldn't remember where many of his accounts were.

- Railroad worker Phineas P Gage was working with some dynamite that exploded unexpectedly and a metre-long iron bar weighing 13 lb (6 kg) went clear through his brain. He remained conscious, but was unable to see out of his left eye. After a while, his sight returned and he fully recovered.

- In November 1972, student skydiver Bob Hail jumped from his plane then discovered that both his main parachute and his back-up parachute had failed. He dropped 3,300 ft (1,006 m) at a rate of 80 mph (129 kph), and smashed into the ground face first. A few moments after landing, however, he got up and walked away with only minor injuries.

- Comedy team Abbott and Costello had an insurance policy to cover themselves financially, in the event they had an argument with each other.

———— THE WORLD AND ITS PEOPLE ————

- A Japanese priest set a kimono on fire in Tokyo in 1657 because it carried bad luck. The flames spread until over 10,000 buildings were destroyed and 100,000 people died.

- Taxi drivers in London are required to pass a training test based on 'The Blue Book', with preparation for this test taking between two and four years. Of 10 drivers who start, eight or nine drop out before completion.

- The most children born from the same mother, at one time, were decaplets. Born in Brazil, in 1946, eight girls and two boys were delivered.

- The most popular topic of public speakers is motivation at 23%, followed by leadership at 17%.

- One lady had her husband's ashes made into an egg timer so that, even in death, he can still 'help' in the kitchen.

- The most popular form of hair removal among women is shaving, with 70% of women who remove hair doing so by shaving.

- All pilots on international flights identify themselves in English, regardless of their country of origin.

—————— **THE WORLD AND ITS PEOPLE** ——————

- The disgraced Lord Jeffrey Archer once worked as a deckchair attendant during the holiday season in Weston-super-Mare in Somerset.

- Karl Marx rarely took a bath and suffered from boils most of his life.

- Early students of forensics hoped that by photographing the eyes of murder victims they would see a reflection of the murderer lingering in the victim's eyes.

- Some odour technicians in the perfume trade have the olfactory skill to distinguish 20,000 odours at 20 levels of intensity.

- Each morning more than a third of all adults hit their alarm clock's 'snooze' button an average of three times before they get up. Those most guilty of snatching some extra sleep are those in the 25–34 age bracket, at 57%.

- Teenagers often have episodes of anger and negativity in which they slam doors and scream tirades, most of these lasting an average of 15 minutes.

- Adults spend an average of 16 times as many hours selecting clothes (145.6 hours a year) as they do on planning their retirement.

THE WORLD AND ITS PEOPLE

- Iraqi terrorist Khay Rahnajet, didn't pay enough postage on a letter bomb. It came back with 'return to sender' stamped on it. Forgetting it was the bomb; he opened it and was blown to bits.

- Peter the Great hated the Kremlin, where, as a child, he had witnessed the brutal torture and murder of his mother's family.

- The shortest human on which there is documented evidence was Pauline Musters of the Netherlands. She measured 12 inches (30 cm) at her birth in 1876, and was 23 inches (58 cm) tall with a weight of 9 lb (4 kg) at her death in 1885.

- Two German motorists each guiding their car at a snail's pace near the centre of the road, due to heavy fog near the town of Guetersloh, had an all-too-literal head-on collision. At the moment of impact their heads were both out of the windows when they smacked together. Both men were hospitalised with severe head injuries, though their cars weren't scratched.

- About 18% of animal owners share their bed with their pets.

- Two animal rights protesters were protesting at the

———— THE WORLD AND ITS PEOPLE ————

cruelty of sending pigs to a slaughterhouse in Bonn.
Suddenly the pigs – all 2,000 of them – escaped through
a broken fence and stampeded, trampling the two
helpless protesters to death.

- Couples who diet while on holiday argue three times
  more often than those who don't; and those who don't
  diet have three times as many romantic interludes.

- Two out of every three women in the world are
  illiterate.

- In Britain, two women were killed in 1999 by lightning
  conducted through their under-wired bras.

- Women who snore are at an increased risk of high blood
  pressure and cardiovascular disease.

- Astronauts Neil Armstrong and Buzz Aldrin ate roast
  turkey from foil packets for their first meal on the moon.

- About 24% of alcoholics die in accidents, falls, fires or
  suicides.

- US Army doctor D W Bliss had the unique role of
  attending to two US presidents after assassins shot them.
  In 1865, he was one of 16 doctors who tried to save

--- **THE WORLD AND ITS PEOPLE** ---

Abraham Lincoln; in 1881, Bliss supervised the care of James Garfield.

- King John did not sign the Magna Carta in 1215, as he could not write his name. Instead he placed his seal on it.

- Notorious bootlegger Al Capone made £34,000,000 during Prohibition.

- One out of 10 people admitted that they would buy an outfit intending to wear it once and return it.

- Only 29% of married couples agree on most political issues.

- It is estimated that 74 billion human beings have been born and died in the last 500,000 years.

- Thirty-nine per cent of people admit that, as guests, they have snooped in their host's medicine cabinets.

- Trying to prevent ageing, Charlie Chaplin, Winston Churchill and Christian Dior all had injections of foetal lamb cells. The process failed.

- In a test of Russian psychic Djuna Davitashvili's powers, a computer randomly selected a San Francisco landmark

———— **THE WORLD AND ITS PEOPLE** ————

for her to predict. However, not only had she managed to predict it correctly six hours before it made the selection, Djuna also gave an incredibly detailed description of the site, though she was 6,000 miles away in Moscow at the time.

- A psychology student in New York rented out her spare room to a carpenter in order to nag him constantly and study his reactions. After weeks of needling, he snapped and beat her repeatedly with an axe, leaving her mentally retarded.

- The average person receives eight birthday cards annually.

- More than 50% of adults say that children should not be paid money for getting good grades in school.

- Robert Todd Lincoln, son of Abraham Lincoln, was present at the assassinations of three presidents: his father's, President Garfield's, and President McKinley's. After the last shooting, he refused ever to attend a state affair again.

- Leonardo da Vinci wrote notebook entries in backwards script, a trick that kept many of his observations from being widely known until decades after his death. It is believed that he was hiding his scientific ideas from the

THE WORLD AND ITS PEOPLE

powerful Roman Catholic Church, whose teachings sometimes disagreed with what Da Vinci observed.

- Peter the Great of Russia was almost 7 ft (2 m) tall.

- On his way home to visit his parents, a Harvard student fell between two rail-road cars at the station in Jersey City, New Jersey, and was rescued by an actor on his way to visit a sister in Philadelphia. The student was Robert Lincoln, heading for 1600 Pennsylvania Avenue. The actor was Edwin Booth, the brother of the man who, a few weeks later, would murder the student's father.

- Six per cent of people that file for bankruptcy do so because they cannot stand bill collectors.

- A flower shop entrepreneur named O'Banion held the greatest ever funeral for a gangster in Chicago. The shop, at the corner of State and Superior Streets, was a front for O'Banion's bootlegging and hijacking operations. Ten thousand mourners were in attendance, and the most expensive wreath, costing $1,000, came from Al Capone, who had ordered that O'Banion be killed.

- King George I could not speak English, as he was born and raised in Germany, so he left the running of the country to his ministers.

THE WORLD AND ITS PEOPLE

- When a thief was surprised while burgling a house in Antwerp, Belgium, he fled out of the back door, clambered over a 9-ft (3 m) wall, dropped down and found himself in the city prison.

- Queen Anne had a transvestite cousin, Lord Cornbury, whom she assigned to be governor of New York and New Jersey.

- About 25% of alcoholics are women.

- Levi Strauss was paid £3.35 in gold dust for his first pair of jeans.

- Adolf Hitler's third-grade school report remarked that Hitler was 'bad tempered' and fancied himself as a leader.

- Robert Peary, discoverer of the North Pole, included a photograph of his nude mistress in a book about his travels.

- The first women flight attendants in 1930 were required to be unmarried, trained nurses, and weigh no more than 115 lb (52 kg).

- One of Napoleon's drinking cups was made from the skull of the famous Italian adventurer Cagliostro.

—————— THE WORLD AND ITS PEOPLE ——————

- When King Edward II was deposed from the throne in the 14th century, there were strict instructions that no one should harm him. To avoid leaving marks on his body when he was murdered, a deer horn was inserted into his rectum then a red-hot poker was placed inside it.

- Pamela Anderson is Canada's Centennial Baby, being the first baby born on the centennial anniversary of Canada's independence.

- A woman weighing less than 100 lb (45 kg) ran a fever of 114°F (45.5°C) and survived without brain damage or physiological after-effects.

- Seventy-five per cent of people who play the car radio while driving also sing along with it.

- While 1950s Hollywood actor Jack Palance was serving in the US Air Corps, during World War II, he was shot down. His plane descended in flames, and although Palance survived the crash, he received severe facial burns that required major plastic surgery.

- Lincoln's assassin, John Wilkes Booth, was a famous actor who belonged to one of the most distinguished theatrical families of the 19th century. He received 100 fan letters a week.

THE WORLD AND ITS PEOPLE

- Orson Welles' ghost is said to haunt Sweet Lady Jane's restaurant in Los Angeles, where customers and employees have reported seeing Welles' caped apparition sitting at his favourite table, often accompanied by the scent of his favourite brandy and cigars.

- French chemist Louis Pasteur had an obsessive fear of dirt and infection. He would never shake hands, would carefully wipe his plate and glass before dining, and would sneak a microscope into friends' houses under his coat and then examine the food they served to make sure it was safe from germs.

- Pope Innocent VIII drank the blood of three young donors thinking it would prevent ageing, and died shortly after.

- Three per cent of adults use toilet paper to clean a child's hands and/or face.

- Tsar Nicholas II considered the construction of an electric fence around Russia and expressed interest in building a bridge across the Bering Straits.

- Andrew Carnegie, one of the richest Americans ever, never carried any cash. He was once sent off a London train because he did not have the fare.

——— THE WORLD AND ITS PEOPLE ———

- Purple is by far the favourite ink colour in pens used by bingo players.

- The average person spends 30 years being angry with a family member.

- Thirty per cent of all marriages occur because of friendship.

- Seventy per cent of women would rather have chocolate than sex.

- Before going into the music business, Frank Zappa was a greetings-card designer.

- University graduates live longer than people who did not complete school.

- Composer Richard Wagner was known to dress in historical costumes while writing his operas.

- In 1981, near Pisa, 42-year-old Romolo Ribolla was so depressed about not being able to find a job, he sat in his kitchen with a gun in his hand threatening to kill himself. His wife pleaded for him not to do it, and after about an hour he burst into tears and threw the gun to the floor. It went off and killed his wife.

THE WORLD AND ITS PEOPLE

- Humphrey Bogart's ashes are in an urn that also contains a small gold whistle. Lauren Bacall had the whistle inscribed, *'If you need anything, just whistle'* – the words she spoke to him in their first film together, *To Have and Have Not* (1944).

- Of devout coffee drinkers, about 62% of those who are 35 to 49 years of age say they become upset if they don't have a cup of coffee at their regular time. Only 50% of those under age 35 become upset.

- Leonardo da Vinci was the first person to suggest using contact lenses for vision, in 1508.

- Napoleon's haemorrhoids contributed to his defeat at Waterloo, as they prevented him from surveying the battlefield on horseback.

- The lightest human adult ever was Lucia Xarate, from Mexico. At the age of 17, in 1889, she weighed 4 lb 11 oz (2.13 kg).

- Isaac Newton's only recorded utterance while he was a Member of Parliament was a request to open the window.

- Sixty per cent of men spit in public.

THE WORLD AND ITS PEOPLE

- Men who are exposed to a lot of toxic chemicals, high heat and unusual pressures, such as jet pilots and deep-sea divers, are more prone to father girls than boys.

- Cleopatra tested the efficacy of her poisons by giving them to slaves.

- Only about 30% of teenage males consistently apply sun-protection lotion compared with 46% of female teens.

- American showman P T Barnum had his obituary published before his death.

- Lawrence of Arabia's ghost is said to be heard riding his motorbike near his house in Dorset, England, where he died in a motorbike accident.

- Alcoholics are twice as likely to confess a drinking problem to a computer than to a doctor.

- With 382,650 babies being born each day and 144,902 people dying daily, the world population increases by about 237,748 people a day.

- Italian composer Gioacchino Antonio Rossini covered himself with blankets when he composed, and could only find inspiration by getting profoundly drunk.

-------- **THE WORLD AND ITS PEOPLE** --------

- Henry Ford was obsessed with soy-beans. He once wore a suit and tie made from soy-based material, served a 16-course meal made entirely from soy-beans, and ordered many Ford auto parts to be made from soy-derived plastic.

- Albert Einstein reportedly had a huge crush on film star Marilyn Monroe.

- People who eat fresh fruit daily have 24% fewer heart attacks and 32% fewer strokes than those that don't.

- Marcel Proust worked in bed, and only in a soundproof room.

- King Charles VIII of France was obsessed with the idea of being poisoned. As his phobia grew, the monarch ate so little that he died of malnutrition.

- In 1979, David Booth had a series of recurring nightmares about a plane crashing, and on 25 May 1979 his premonitions came true. Departing from Chicago's O'Hare Airport, a DC-10 flew half a mile then turned on its side and slammed into the ground, exploding on impact. The 272 people on board died. Booth's dreams started on 16 May, and continued for seven nights. Having seen the name of the airline in his dreams, Booth went and told people in authority at the airport. They

──── THE WORLD AND ITS PEOPLE ────

made notes of what he'd told them, but claimed they couldn't just ground a whole airline, so the planes went on as usual – and Booth's nightmares came true.

- The spirit of silent-screen star Rudolph Valentino is said to haunt Paramount Studios in Hollywood, with the Sheik's shimmering spectre seen floating among old garments in the costume department.

- After the death of Alexander the Great, his remains were preserved in a huge crock of honey.

- 3.9% per cent of women say they don't wear underwear.

- Albert Einstein was reluctant to sign autographs, and charged people a dollar before signing anything. He gave the dollars to charity.

- It's been estimated that an opera singer burns an average of more than two calories per minute during a performance.

- King Alfonso of Spain was so tone-deaf that he had one man in his employ known as the 'Anthem Man'. The man's duty was to tell the king to stand up whenever the Spanish national anthem was played, as the monarch couldn't recognise it.

—— THE WORLD AND ITS PEOPLE ——

- Lady Diana Spencer was the first Englishwoman commoner in 300 years to marry an heir to the British throne.

- Elderly women are more likely to live alone than elderly men; 17% of men 65 years or older are living alone, compared with 42% of women the same age.

- As a boy, Charles Darwin was so enamoured with chemistry that his young friends nicknamed him 'Gas'.

- Paul Cézanne was 56 years old when he had his first one-man exhibition.

- Julius Caesar and Dostoyevsky were epileptics.

- Napoleon suffered from ailurophobia, the fear of cats.

- Viscount Horatio Nelson chose to be buried in St Paul's Cathedral in London rather than in the national shrine of Westminster Abbey because he had heard that Westminster was sinking into the Thames River.

- A fierce gust of wind blew 45-year-old Vittorio Luise's car into a river near Naples, Italy, in 1983. He managed to break a window, climb out and swim to shore, where a tree blew over and killed him.

———— THE WORLD AND ITS PEOPLE ————

- Six per cent of motorists said they sometimes leave their keys in the ignition of their unattended car.

- Napoleon Bonaparte was always depicted with his hand inside his jacket because he suffered from 'chronic nervous itching' and often scratched his stomach sores until they bled.

- The younger of Albert Einstein's two sons was a schizophrenic.

- More than 20% of men and 10% of women say they've forgotten their wedding anniversary at least once.

- Catherine II of Russia kept her wigmaker in an iron cage in her bedroom for more than three years.

- One in three male motorists picks his nose while driving.

- The average housewife walks 10 miles (16 km) a day around the house doing her chores. In addition, she walks nearly 4 miles (6 km) and spends 25 hours a year making beds.

- Over 80% of professional boxers have suffered brain damage.

──── THE WORLD AND ITS PEOPLE ────

● Emerson Moser, Crayola's senior crayon maker, revealed upon his retirement that he was blue-green colour-blind and couldn't see all the colours.

● Nearly half of all psychiatrists have been attacked by one of their patients.

● Xerxes, King of Persia, became so angry at the sea when it destroyed his two bridges of boats during a storm, he had his army beat it with sticks.

● The Marquis de Sade was only 5 ft 3 in (about 1.6m) tall.

● Using a fine pen and a microscope, James Zaharee printed Abraham Lincoln's Gettysburg Address on a human hair less than 3 inches (8 cm) long.

● About 25% of all adolescent and adult males never use deodorant.

● Men change their minds two to three times more than women. Women tend to take longer to make a decision, but once they do, they are more likely to stick to it.

● Believing that he could end his wife's incessant nagging by giving her a good scare, Hungarian Jake Fen built an elaborate harness to make it look as if he had hanged

———— THE WORLD AND ITS PEOPLE ————

himself. When his wife came home and saw him, she fainted. Hearing a disturbance, a neighbour came over and, finding what she thought were two corpses, seized the opportunity to loot the place. As she was leaving the room, her arms laden, the outraged and suspended Mr Fen kicked her stoutly on the backside. This so surprised the lady that she dropped dead of a heart attack. Happily, Mr Fen was acquitted of manslaughter and he and his wife were reconciled.

- Only one person walked with Mozart's coffin, from the church to the cemetery, for its burial.

- Some publishers claim that science-fiction readers are better educated than the average book buyer.

- Jeff Bezos, founder of Amazon.com, shoots at least one snapshot a day to chronicle his life.

- Women comprise less than 2% of the total death row population in America's prisons.

- Martha Jane Burke, better known as Calamity Jane, was married twelve times.

- Telephone inventor Alexander Graham Bell had an odd habit of drinking his soup through a glass straw.

-------- **THE WORLD AND ITS PEOPLE** --------

● Victoria Woodhall, the radical feminist who ran for the US presidency in 1872, feared that she would die if she went to bed in her old age. She spent the last four years of her life sitting in a chair.

● Jesse James would run back home to his mother following a crime. His obsessive love for his mother extended to him marrying a woman named Zerelda, the same name as his mother's and one that was uncommon in the 1800s.

● In 1983, a woman was laid out in her coffin, presumed dead of heart disease. As mourners watched, she suddenly sat up. Her daughter dropped dead of fright.

● When he was a boy, Thomas Edison suffered a permanent hearing loss following a head injury. One of his ears was pulled roughly as he was being lifted aboard a moving train.

● While sleeping, one man in eight snores, and one in 10 grinds his teeth.

● The most celebrated levitator in history was St Joseph of Copertino, a dim-witted monk who would allegedly soar into the air whenever he felt religious ecstasy. He had no control over his 'flights', which could last for

THE WORLD AND ITS PEOPLE

minutes and were attested to by scores of witnesses, including the Pope.

- Mozart once composed a piano piece that required a player to use two hands and a nose in order to hit all the correct notes.

- When Napoleon wore black silk handkerchiefs around his neck during a battle, he always won. At Waterloo, he wore a white cravat and lost the battle.

- The Roman emperor Nero married his male slave Scorus in a public ceremony.

- Twenty-five per cent of women think money makes a man sexier.

- Pablo Picasso was born dead. His midwife abandoned him on a table, leaving Picasso's uncle to bring him to life with a lung full of cigar smoke.

- Tchaikovsky was financed by a wealthy widow for 13 years. At her request, they never met.

- The great lover and adventurer Casanova was earning his living as a librarian for a count in Bohemia when he died at age 73.

THE WORLD AND ITS PEOPLE

- Today, 5.9 billion people live on the earth.

- The first person other than royalty to be portrayed on a British stamp was William Shakespeare, in 1964.

- Offered a new pen to write with, 97% of all people will write their own name.

- There are 106 boys born for every 100 girls.

- When Errol Flynn appeared as a contestant on the mid-1950s TV quiz show *The Big Surprise*, he was questioned about sailing and won $30,000.

- The world's population grows by 100 million each year.

- 950 million people in the world are malnourished.

- The men who served as guards along the Great Wall of China in the Middle Ages were often born on the wall, grew up there, married there, died there, and were buried within it. Many of these guards never left the wall in their entire lives.

- Actor Montgomery Clift is said to haunt room number 928 of the Roosevelt Hotel in Hollywood, which was home to him for three months while filming *From Here*

——— THE WORLD AND ITS PEOPLE ———

to Eternity (1953). Hotel guests and employees have reported sensing the actor's presence, or have heard him reciting his lines and playing the trumpet. One guest felt a hand patting her shoulder, while others claim to feel cold spots in the room.

- After Frank Lahainer died in March 1995, in Palm Beach, Florida, his widow Gianna had him embalmed and stored for 40 days at a funeral home. It seemed that Frank, worth $300 million, died at an inconvenient time: it was the middle of Palm Beach's social season, and Gianna didn't want to miss any of the parties.

- Nuns have an average life expectancy of 77 years, the longest of any group in the United States.

- St George, the patron saint of England, never actually visited England.

- To help create her signature sexy walk, actress Marilyn Monroe sawed off part of the heel of one shoe.

- After his death, the body of Pope Formosus was dug up and tried for various crimes.

- As the official taste-tester for Edy's Grand Ice Cream, John Harrison had his taste buds insured for $1 million.

———— THE WORLD AND ITS PEOPLE ————

- Ancient Roman gladiators performed product endorsements, as a result of their immense public appeal.

- Cleopatra was part Macedonian, part Greek and part Iranian. She was not an Egyptian.

- There are currently six reigning queens in Europe. They are: Queen Elizabeth II of the United Kingdom; Queen Sofia of Spain; Queen Beatrix of The Netherlands; Queen Margrethe II of Denmark; Queen Silvia of Sweden; and Queen Fabiola of Belgium.

- A man hit by a car in New York in 1977 got up uninjured, but lay back down in front of the car when a bystander told him to pretend he was hurt so he could collect insurance money. The car rolled forward and crushed him to death.

- Julius Caesar, Martin Luther and Jonathan Swift all suffered from Ménière's disease. It is a disorder of the hearing and balance senses, causing progressive deafness and attacks of tinnitus and vertigo.

- King Mithridates VI was so afraid of assassination by poisoning; he gave himself small doses of poison each day in the hope that he would naturally build up a resistance to poisons. It was so successful that when the

-------- **THE WORLD AND ITS PEOPLE** --------

Romans invaded in 63 BC, instead of being captured he tried to commit suicide, but the poison he took had no effect on him. Eventually the king ordered a slave to kill him with his sword.

- Johann Sebastian Bach once walked 230 miles (370 km) to hear the organist at Lubeck in Germany.

- Adolf Hitler was fascinated by hands. In his library there was a well-thumbed book containing pictures and drawings of hands belonging to famous people throughout history. He particularly liked to show his guests how closely his own hands resembled those of Frederick the Great, one of his heroes.

- Handel wrote the score of his 'Messiah' in just over three weeks.

- US actor Larry Hagman didn't allow smoking on the set of TV serial *Dallas*.

- St John was the only one of the Twelve Apostles to die a natural death.

- The pioneering scientist Marie Curie was not allowed to become a member of the prestigious French Academy because she was a woman.

-------- **THE WORLD AND ITS PEOPLE** --------

- In 1994, Los Angeles police arrested a man for dressing as the Grim Reaper – complete with scythe – and standing outside the windows of old people's homes, staring in.

- The composer Richard Wagner was vegetarian, and once published a diatribe against 'the abominable practice of flesh eating'.

- Nazi Adolf Eichmann was originally a travelling salesman for the Vacuum Oil Company of Austria.

- During the 17th century, the Sultan of Turkey ordered that his entire harem of women be drowned and replaced with a new one.

- Henry VII was the only British king to be crowned on the field of battle

- Ludwig van Beethoven was once arrested for vagrancy.

- In 1759, Emmanuel Swedenborg, speaking to a reception full of local notables in Gothenburg, described in vivid detail the progress of a disastrous fire that was sweeping through Stockholm, 300 miles (483 km) away. At six o'clock he told them the fire had just broken out; at eight he told them it had been extinguished only three

———— THE WORLD AND ITS PEOPLE ————

doors from his home. Two days later, a messenger from Stockholm confirmed every detail.

- When Richard II died, in 1400, a hole was left in the side of his tomb so that people could touch his royal head. However, 376 years later, it is said that a schoolboy took advantage of this and stole his jaw-bone.

- Julius Caesar wore a laurel wreath to cover the onset of baldness.

- Blackbird, Chief of the Omaha Indians, was buried sitting on his favourite horse.

- Prime Minister William Gladstone, as a result of his strong Puritan impulses, kept a selection of whips in his cellar with which he regularly chastised himself.

- Irving Berlin composed 3,000 songs in his lifetime but couldn't read music.

- The Winchester Mansion, in San José, California, was built by Sara Winchester, the widow of gun manufacturer William Winchester. She had been told by a psychic to build a house large enough to house the souls of all those who had been killed by Winchester guns. With stairways and doors that go nowhere, secret rooms and

——— THE WORLD AND ITS PEOPLE ———

passages, and elevators that only go up one floor, some believe that Sara had the house built in a confusing way so that the spirits wouldn't be able to find her and seek revenge. Obsessed with the number 13, every night at the stroke of midnight she would sit down to dinner at a table set for 13 people, even though alone. The house also had 13 bathrooms, stairways with 13 steps, and so on. Her superstitions meant that she would never give her workmen the day off, afraid that the day she stopped building she would die. One day, however, after many complaints, she finally gave her staff a day off, and that is the day she died.

- It is believed that Handel haunts his former London home. Many who have entered Handel's bedroom, where he died in 1759, have reported a tall, dark shape and a strong smell of perfume. Roman Catholic priests have performed exorcisms in their bid to clear the house of all spirits before it becomes a museum that will be open to the public.

- China uses 45 billion chopsticks per year, using 25 million trees to make them.

- President Kaunda of Zambia once threatened to resign if his fellow countrymen didn't stop drinking so much alcohol.

THE WORLD AND ITS PEOPLE

- There are more than 150 million sheep in Australia but only 17 million people, while in New Zealand there are only 4 million people compared with 70 million sheep.

- The names of all the continents end with the letter they start with.

- In Holland, you can be fined for not using a shopping basket at a grocery store.

- On every continent there is a city called Rome.

- The oldest inhabited city is Damascus, Syria.

- The first city in the world to have a population of more than one million was London, which today is the 13th most populated city.

- The Atlantic Ocean is saltier than the Pacific Ocean.

- Kilts are not native to Scotland. They originated in France.

- One-third of Taiwanese funeral processions include a stripper.

- It is illegal to own a red car in Shanghai, China.

---------- **THE WORLD AND ITS PEOPLE** ----------

- Antarctica is the only land on our planet that is not owned by any country.

- There is now a cash machine at McMurdo Station in Antarctica, which has a winter population of 200 people.

- Major earthquakes have hit Japan on 1 September 827, 1 September 859, 1 September 1185, 1 September 1649 and 1 September 1923.

- There are 92 known cases of nuclear bombs lost at sea.

- In Nepal, cow dung is used for medicinal purposes.

- All the earth's continents, except Antarctica, are wider at the north than in the south.

- There are no rental cars in Bermuda.

- The richest country in the world is Switzerland, while Mozambique is the poorest.

- Until 1920, Canada was planning on invading the United States.

- In 1956, only 8% of British households had a refrigerator.

THE WORLD AND ITS PEOPLE

- In India, people are legally allowed to marry a dog.

- The ancient Egyptians trained baboons to wait on tables.

- One day in 1892, residents of Paderborn, Germany, witnessed the appearance of an odd-looking yellow cloud. From it fell not only a fierce rain, but also mussels.

- Mount Everest is a foot higher today than it was a century ago, and it is believed to still be growing.

- Greenland has more ice on it than Iceland does, while Iceland has more grass and trees than Greenland.

- The country of Tanzania has an island called Mafia.

- Panama is the only place in the world where someone can see the sun rise over the Pacific Ocean and set over the Atlantic.

- In Poland, a brewery developed a plumbing problem in which beer was accidentally pumped into the incoming water supply. It meant that residents of the town got free beer on tap for one day.

- The Kingdom of Tonga, in the South Pacific, once issued a stamp shaped like a banana.

THE WORLD AND ITS PEOPLE

- A toy available to Japanese children is a small plastic atom bomb.

- Mount Athos, in northern Greece, calls itself an independent country and has a male-only population of about 4,000. No females of any kind, including animals, are allowed. There are 20 monasteries within a space of 20 miles (32 km).

- In Cyprus, there is one cinema per every eight people.

- Two hundred and thirty people died when Moradabad, India, was bombed with giant balls of hail over 2 inches (5 cm) in diameter.

- A church steeple in Germany was struck by lightning and destroyed on 18 April 1599. The members of the church rebuilt it, but it was hit by lightning three more times between then and 1783, and rebuilt again and again. Every time it was hit, the date was 18 April.

- Monaco issued a postage stamp honouring Franklin D Roosevelt, but his picture on the stamp showed six fingers on his left hand.

- The most commonplace name in Britain is Newton, which occurs 150 times.

--------- **THE WORLD AND ITS PEOPLE** ---------

- China has more English speakers than the United States.

- The Toltecs, seventh-century native Mexicans, went into battle with wooden swords so as not to kill their enemies.

- In 1821, stones fell on a house in Truro, Cornwall. The local mayor even visited the house, but was unnerved by the rattling of the walls and roof due to the falling stones. Called in to help, the military was unable to determine the source of the stones, and five days later the fall was still going on.

- Belgium is the only country that has never imposed censorship laws on adult films.

- Freelance Dutch prostitutes have to charge sales tax, but can write off items such as condoms and beds.

- The average court fine for drunk driving in Denmark is one month's salary of the convicted.

- People in Sweden, Japan and Canada are more likely to know the population of the United States than are Americans.

- About 10% of the workforce in Egypt are under 12 years of age.

———— THE WORLD AND ITS PEOPLE ————

- The Netherlands is credited with having the most bikes in the world. One bike per person is the national average, with an estimated 16 million bicycles nation-wide.

- On a summer's evening in Edinburgh, 1849, there was a loud clap of thunder, after which a large and irregularly shaped mass of ice, estimated to be around 20 ft (6 m) in circumference, crashed to earth near a farmhouse.

- The average worker in Japan reportedly takes only half of their earned vacation time each year.

- The Amazon River's flow is 12 times that of the Mississippi. The South American river disgorges as much water in a day as the Thames carries past London in a year.

- Georgia is the world's top pecan producer.

- People in Siberia often buy milk frozen on a stick.

- The population of Colombia doubles every 22 years.

- Sweden is the biggest user of ketchup, spending £2.25 per person a year on it. Australia is the second highest user, spending £1.35 a year, and the United States and Canada are joint-third, spending £1.22 a year. The

─────── **THE WORLD AND ITS PEOPLE** ───────

ketchup expenditure of other countries is as follows: Germany £0.95, United Kingdom £0.90, Poland and Japan £0.77, France £0.65, and Russia £0.50.

- Eighty per cent of the Australian population live in the cities along the coast.

- The most common name for a pub in Britain is 'The Red Lion'.

- Among the shortest people in the world are the Mbuti Pygmies of the Congo River basin, where the men reach an average of 4 ft 6 in (1.36 m) tall.

- In Tokyo, a bicycle is faster than a car for most trips of less than 50 minutes.

- The world's longest escalator is in Ocean Park, Hong Kong. With a length of 745 ft (227 m), the escalator boasts a vertical rise of 377 ft (115 m).

- There is 1 mile (1.6 km) of rail-road track in Belgium for every 1 $^1/_2$ square miles (3.8 square kilometres) of land.

- Fifty per cent of the adult Dutch population has never flown in a plane, and 28% admitted a fear of flying.

—— THE WORLD AND ITS PEOPLE ——

- The tallest sand dunes in the world are in the Sahara desert. The dunes have enough sand in them to bury the Great Pyramids of Egypt and the Eiffel Tower.

- The most visited cemetery in the world is Cimetière du Père-Lachaise, in Paris. Established in 1805, it contains the tombs of over one million people, including: composer Chopin; singer Edith Piaf; writers Oscar Wilde, Molière, Balzac, Marcel Proust and Gertrude Stein; artists David, Delacroix, Pissarro, Seurat and Modigliani; actors Sarah Bernhardt, Simone Signoret and Yves Montand; and dancer Isadora Duncan. The most visited tomb is that of the Doors' former lead singer, Jim Morrison.

- Asia has the greatest number of working children, totalling 45 million. Africa is second, with 24 million.

- There are more than 23,000 cabbies working in London. All are self-employed and none has a police record.

- On some Pacific islands, shark teeth are used to make skin tattoos.

- In Japan, some restaurants serve smaller portions to women, even though the charge is the same as a man's portion.

———— THE WORLD AND ITS PEOPLE ————

● The Japanese cremate 93% of their dead, compared with Great Britain, at 67%, and the United States, at just over 12%.

● Approximately one-third of Greenland, the world's largest island, is national park.

● Kulang, China, runs seven centres for recycled toothpicks. People bringing used toothpicks to the recycling centres are paid the equivalent of 35 cents per pound weight.

● Floor-cleaning products in Venezuela have 10 times the pine fragrance of British floor cleaners, as Venezuelan women won't buy a weaker fragrance. They wet-mop their tile floors twice a day, leaving windows and doors open so the scent can waft out to the street and send the message that their houses are clean.

● Windsor Castle is home to the ghosts of King Henry VIII, Queen Elizabeth I, King Charles I and King George III. King Henry is supposed to haunt the cloisters near the Deanery with ghostly groans and the sound of dragging footsteps.

● All education through the university level is free in the Eastern European nation of Azerbaijan.

———— THE WORLD AND ITS PEOPLE ————

● Canada is the largest importer of American cars.

● No one knows how many people live in Bhutan, a small independent kingdom on the slopes of the Himalayas. As of 1975, no census has ever been taken.

● On average, 51 cars a year overshoot and drive into the canals of Amsterdam.

● London cabbies estimate their average driving speed to be 9 mph (14 kph) due to increasing traffic congestion.

● The area of Greater Tokyo – meaning the city, its port, Yokohama, and the suburban prefectures of Saitama, Chiba and Kanagawa – contains less than 4% of Japan's land area, but fully one-quarter of its 123-plus million people.

● Based on population, Chinese Mandarin is the most commonly spoken language in the world. Spanish follows second, English third, and Bengali fourth.

● At about 200 million years of age, the Atlantic Ocean is the youngest of the world's oceans.

● In Finland, the awards for best children's fairy-tales by children are held on 18 October, known as Satu's Day. The international competition for children ages 7 to 13

THE WORLD AND ITS PEOPLE

has been held since 1993, and its rules are translated into five languages.

- Britain is roughly nine times more densely populated than America, with 588 people per square mile as compared with America's 65 people per square mile.

- In China there are 600 bicycles for every car.

- At London's Drury Lane Theatre, sightings of a ghost described as a soft green glow, or a handsome young man, have been numerous. During renovation in the late 1970s, workers found a skeleton with the remnants of a grey riding coat and a knife sticking out of its ribs. The deceased was found to be a young ghost hunter who was murdered in 1780.

- Among the tallest people in the world are the Tutsi from Rwanda and Burundi, in central Africa, with the men averaging 6 ft (1.8 m) tall.

- At 12,000 ft (3,658 m) above sea level, there is barely enough oxygen in La Paz, Bolivia, to support combustion. The city is nearly fireproof.

- Of the 15,000-odd known species of orchids in the world, 3,000 of them can be found in Brazil.

THE WORLD AND ITS PEOPLE

- Given one square metre per person, all the people in the world could fit on the Indonesian island of Bali, if they stood shoulder to shoulder.

- In a recent five-year period, 24 residents of Tokyo died while bowing to other people.

- Australia is home to 500 species of coral.

- A Chinese soap hit it big with consumers in Asia, claiming that users would lose weight by washing with it. The soap was promptly banned.

- One in five people in the world's population lives in China.

- In Wales, there are more sheep than people. The human population for Wales is 2,921,000, with approximately 5,000,000 sheep.

- The country with the most post offices is India, with over 152,792.

- In Switzerland, when a male reaches 20 years of age, he is required to undergo 15 weeks of military training. Over the next few decades, he has to attend training camps until he has accrued 300 to 1,300 days of active

———THE WORLD AND ITS PEOPLE———

service. Swiss men who live abroad don't have to serve in the Swiss military, but they are required to pay 2% of their income in the form of a military exemption tax. Men who don't qualify for military service also pay the tax, but women aren't required to pay the tax, nor are they expected to serve in the Swiss army.

- Ireland boasts the highest per capita consumption of cereal in the world — 15 lb (6.8 kg) per person annually.

- The popular American comic strip 'Peanuts' is known as 'Radishes' in Denmark.

- In Cupar, Scotland, in June of 1842, women hanging clothing on clothes-lines in an open area heard a sudden detonation and the clothes shot upward. Eventually, some of the clothing did fall back to the ground, but others kept ascending until it disappeared. Even odder, the clothes were carried off to the north, but chimney smoke in that area indicated that the wind was moving to the south.

- The country of Togo has the lowest crime rate in the world, with an average of just 11 reported crimes annually for every 100,000 of the population.

- The state bird of Texas is the mockingbird.

———— THE WORLD AND ITS PEOPLE ————

- Contrary to many reports, the Eisenhower Interstate System does *not* require that one mile in every five must be straight in the United States. The claim that these straight sections are usable as airstrips in times of war or other emergencies does not exist in any federal legislation. Korea and Sweden *do* use some of their roads as military airstrips.

- There are more than 100 offences that carry the death penalty in Iran.

- Airborne sand from the Sahara Desert has been picked up 2,000 miles (3,216 km) over the ocean.

- With an exchange rate running at an average of 428,287.55 Ukrainian karbovanets to the dollar, total assets of just US $6 will qualify a person as a Ukrainian millionaire.

- Britain's Lightwater Valley Theme Park has the longest roller coaster in the world, The Ultimate.

- Close to 72% of Australia's Aboriginals live in towns and cities.

- Over the many centuries of living in the Arctic, Eskimos' bodies have adapted to the cold. Eskimos tend to be

———— **THE WORLD AND ITS PEOPLE** ————

short and squat, which brings their arms and legs closer to the heart, so there is less danger of freezing. Extra fat around the torso protects their internal organs from the cold. The metabolism of Eskimos is also set a little higher than that of other peoples'. As a result, they burn their food faster to stay warm. Their veins and arteries are also arranged to carry more warming blood to their hands.

- The full name for Britain, The United Kingdom of Great Britain and Northern Ireland, is the third longest country name in the world.

- Greenland ranks as the country with the highest percentage of smoking teenagers, with 56% of 15-year-old boys and 45% of 15-year-old girls smoking a cigarette daily.

- The country of Yemen has the world's highest fertility rate (average number of births per woman), at 7.6, while Switzerland has the world's lowest, at 1.5.

- Studies show that Chinese babies cry less and are more easily consoled than American babies.

- The Gulf Stream carries about 30 billion gallons (136 billion litres) of water every second – six times as much water as all the rivers in the world.

THE WORLD AND ITS PEOPLE

- Roughly 40% of the population of the underdeveloped world is under 15 years old.

- London Heathrow Airport is the busiest international airport in the world, typically handling over 44 million international passengers a year. If you include domestic passengers, the total is about 51 million customers, which ranks fourth in the world.

- In terms of beer consumption, Britain is ranked seventh in the world, with the average Brit drinking 180 pints a year. The heaviest drinkers are in the Czech Republic, consuming 281 pints a year.

- Japan is expected to overtake Sweden as the world's most geriatric nation by the year 2005.

- Japan is the largest harvester of seafood in the world, taking 15% of the world's total catch.

- When T E Lawrence returned from Arabia, he tried to become anonymous, often using the false names Ross and Shaw.

- In Thailand, the bodies of monks are preserved, once deceased, and placed on public display. However, in an atmosphere of smog, humidity and heat, these corpses

THE WORLD AND ITS PEOPLE

still have teeth, hair and skin decades after their deaths, even though no special techniques are used to preserve the bodies.

- Throughout the South Pacific, no building is taller than the tallest palm tree.

- Visitors who wish to return to Rome must throw a coin into the Trevi fountain.

- Per capita, the Irish eat more chocolate than Americans, Swedes, Danes, French and Italians.

- Portugal was the first European country to start building its overseas empire.

- There are castles on the River Rhine in Germany called the Cat and Mouse castles.

- Munich has a chiming clock on its medieval town hall with two tiers of dancing and jousting figures that emerge twice daily.

- The Parthenon, in Athens, is built in the Doric style of architecture.

- Stockholm is known as the 'Venice of the North'.

THE WORLD AND ITS PEOPLE

- More than 1,000 languages are spoken in Africa.

- Shanghai, China, is sometimes called 'the Paris of the East' and 'the Whore of China'.

- The Spanish Steps are actually in Rome.

- There are no rivers in Saudi Arabia.

- Nearly half the population of Alaska live in one city, Anchorage.

- The Ainu are the aboriginal people of Japan.

- The women of the Tiwi tribe in the South Pacific are married at birth.

- The bulk of the island of Tenerife is the volcanic mountain, Mount Teide.

- The Canary Islands were once known as Blessed or Fortunate Isles.

- Mount Aso, in Japan, is the world's largest volcanic crater.

- Approximately a quarter of the world's population is made up of Chinese.

THE WORLD AND ITS PEOPLE

- Denmark has the oldest flag in the world.

- China has the most borders with other countries.

- Polish people use zloty ('golden') as currency.

- The Romany people were wrongly thought to have come from Egypt, earning them the nickname 'Gypsies'.

- Zaire was formerly known as the Belgian Congo.

- Nicaragua is the largest and most sparsely populated state in Central America.

- Columbia's largest export is cocaine.

- Himalayas means 'abode of snow'.

- The Karakoram mountain range is known as the 'roof of the world'.

- Venice consists of 118 islands linked by 400 bridges.

- France is sometimes called the 'Hexagon' because it is roughly six-sided.

- Socrates taught Plato, who in turn taught Aristotle.

———— THE WORLD AND ITS PEOPLE ————

- British Prime Minister William Gladstone's middle name was Ewart.

- Ronald Reagan was a sports commentator before becoming a Hollywood actor.

- Four American presidents were assassinated while in office: Lincoln, McKinley, Garfield and Kennedy.

- Ronald Reagan once advertised Chesterfield cigarettes.

- Linus Pauling is the only man ever to win two individual Nobel prizes; one for peace, the other for chemistry.

- British Prime Minister Edward Heath captained the winning team in the yacht *Morning Cloud* in the 1969 Sydney to Hobart race.

- President Lincoln's advisor during the Civil War, Frederick Douglass, was born a slave.

- American astronaut John Glenn became a US Senator in 1974 but was unsuccessful in his bid to become a Democratic presidential candidate.

- John F Kennedy was the first Catholic President of the United States.

THE WORLD AND ITS PEOPLE

- Robin Hood became a titled gentleman called the Earl of Huntingdon.

- Fellow prison inmates killed the American serial sex murderer Jeffrey Dahmer in 1994.

- Christian Barnard performed the first heart transplant in the 1960s.

- JFK is buried at Arlington National Cemetery, Virginia.

- Nathuran Godse assassinated Gandhi in 1948.

- Malcolm X's daughter Qubilah Bahiyah Shabazz was charged with allegedly hiring a hitman to kill the leader of Nation of Islam.

- When Neil Armstrong and Buzz Aldrin walked on the moon in 1969, Michael Collins was left behind in the command module.

- O J Simpson checks into hotels under the name D H Lawrence.

- John F Kennedy represented Massachusetts as senator.

- Stella Rimington was the first woman to head MI5.

———THE WORLD AND ITS PEOPLE———

- Ronald Reagan's Scottish terriers were called Scotch and Soda.

14

LANGUAGE AND
LITERATURE

LANGUAGE AND LITERATURE

- The word 'palace' comes from the name of one of the hills in the ancient city of Rome – the Palatine Hill.

- *The Times* was nicknamed 'The Thunderer'.

- Britain's oldest Sunday newspaper is the *Observer*.

- The word 'education' is based on the Latin '*educo*', which means 'to draw out'.

- James Bond author Ian Fleming also wrote the children's novel *Chitty Chitty Bang Bang*.

- Mary Ann Evans is the real name of George Eliot.

- American poet Emily Dickinson was a recluse by the age of 30, dressing only in white and carrying on friendships through correspondence.

- A full-page colour advert in American *Vogue*, seen by 1.2 million, costs $80,000.

- Margaret Mitchell wrote the novel *Gone with the Wind*, as she was bored while recuperating from a sprained ankle.

- The word 'taxi' is spelled the same in English, German, French, Swedish and Portuguese.

LANGUAGE AND LITERATURE

- Danielle Steel is a descendant of the Löwenbrau brewery family and ran a PR firm called Supergirls before becoming a novelist.

- Agatha Christie created a mystery herself by disappearing for a fortnight in 1926, only to be discovered at a Harrogate hotel.

- Etymology is the study of the history of words.

- Lewis Carroll was a mathematics professor at Oxford University.

- D H Lawrence's novel *Lady Chatterley's Lover* was the subject of an obscenity trial in Britain in 1959.

- The Soviet Union banned Sir Arthur Conan Doyle's *The Adventures of Sherlock Holmes* because of the book's references to occultism and spiritualism.

- The classic tale of *Little Red Riding Hood* was banned in the town of Empire, California, as the book cover showed a bottle of wine in Little Red Riding Hood's basket. The local school board was afraid that the story encouraged the drinking of alcohol.

- Conchology is the study of shells.

--------- **LANGUAGE AND LITERATURE** ---------

- Hans Christian Andersen's *Wonder Stories* was banned from children's reading lists in Illinois, with the book stamped 'For Adult Readers' to make it 'impossible for children to obtain smut'.

- The Indian epic poem the *Mahabharata* is eight times longer than the Greek epic poems the *Iliad* and the *Odyssey* combined.

- Scarlett O'Hara, Margaret Mitchell's *Gone with the Wind* heroine, was originally given the name Pansy.

- There are more than 40,000 characters in Chinese script.

- In Latin, the term '*lego*' means 'I put together' or 'I assemble'.

- The phrase 'in the limelight' originates from chemist Robert Hare discovering that a blowpipe flame acting upon a block of calcium oxide (lime) produces a brilliant white light that could be used to illuminate theatre stages.

- Winnie, from A A Milne's story *Winnie the Pooh*, was named after a bear at the London Zoo. The animal had been born in Canada but was brought to London in 1914 as the mascot of a Canadian regiment.

———— **LANGUAGE AND LITERATURE** ————

- A 'keeper' is the loop on a belt that holds the loose end.

- There are three sets of letters on the standard typewriter and computer keyboards, which are in alphabetical order reading left to right. They are f-g-h, j-k-l, and o-p.

- The *Boston Nation*, a newspaper published in Ohio during the mid-19th century, had pages 7 1/2 feet (2 m) long and 5 1/2 feet (1.6 m) wide. It required two people to hold the paper in a proper reading position.

- The original title of Jane Austen's novel *Pride and Prejudice* was 'First Impression'.

- Lord Alfred Tennyson wrote a 6,000-word epic poem when he was 12 years old.

- A 'vamp' is the upper front top of a shoe.

- Created by author Astrid Lindgren, the children's book character Pippi Longstocking's full name is Pippilolta Provisionia Gaberdina Dandeliona Ephraimsdaughter Longstocking.

- Jacqueline Susann's best-selling novel *Valley of the Dolls* was originally titled 'They Don't Build Statues to Businessmen'.

LANGUAGE AND LITERATURE

- The expression 'knuckle down' originated with marbles – players put knuckles to the ground for their best shots.

- Due to a suggestive illustration that might encourage children to break dishes so they don't have to dry them, Shel Silverstein's children's book *A Light in the Attic* was banned in the US.

- Fagin, the sinister villain in Charles Dickens' *Oliver Twist*, was also the name of Dickens' best friend, Bob Fagin.

- All the proceeds earned from James M Barrie's book *Peter Pan* were bequeathed to the Great Ormond Street Hospital for Sick Children in London.

- Almost half the newspapers in the world are published in the United States and Canada.

- Anyone writing a letter to the *New York Times* has one chance in 21 of having the letter published. Letter writers to the *Washington Post* do significantly better, with one letter out of eight finding its way to print.

- In *Gulliver's Travels*, Jonathan Swift described the two moons of Mars, Phobos and Deimos, giving their exact size and speeds of rotation. He did this more than a hundred years before either moon was discovered.

——— **LANGUAGE AND LITERATURE** ———

- The French Academy took 297 years, from 1635 to 1932, to write a grammar book of 263 pages. When finally published, it contained 50 typographical errors.

- The hero in Robert Burns' poem *Tam O'Shanter* gave name to the flat Scottish wool cap with a pompom at its centre.

- According to experts, the fungi that feed on old paper may be mildly hallucinogenic. Writing in the British medical journal *The Lancet*, one of Britain's leading mycologists (fungus experts) Dr R J Hay said that the 'fungal hallucinogens' in old books could lead to an 'enhancement of enlightenment' in readers. 'The source of inspiration for many great literary figures may have been nothing more than a quick sniff of mouldy books,' wrote Hay.

- The first advertisement printed in English in 1477 offered a prayer book. The advert was published by William Caxton on his press in Westminster Abbey. No price was mentioned, only that the book was 'good chepe'.

- Of all the professionals in the United States, journalists are credited with having the largest vocabulary – approximately 20,000 words.

LANGUAGE AND LITERATURE

- Huckleberry Finn's remedy for warts was swinging a dead cat in a graveyard at night.

- On average, clergymen, lawyers, and doctors each have 15,000 words in their vocabulary. Skilled workers who haven't had a college education know between 5,000 and 7,000 words, and farm labourers know about 1,600.

- The Procrastinators' Club of America sends news to its members under the mast-head 'Last Month's Newsletter'.

- The piece that protrudes from the top end of an umbrella is called a 'ferrule'. The word 'ferrule' is also used to describe the piece of metal that holds a rubber eraser on a pencil.

- The little bits of paper left over when holes are punched in data cards or tape are called 'chad'.

- 'Brontology' is the study of thunder.

- Victor Hugo wrote *The Hunchback of Notre Dame* in just six months and, it is said, with a single bottle of ink.

- *Harriet the Spy*, by Louise Fitzhugh, has been banned in parts of the US for teaching children to lie, spy, talk back and curse.

———— LANGUAGE AND LITERATURE ————

- More than 63 million *Star Trek* books, in more than 15 languages, are in print; 13 are sold every minute in the United States.

- The smallest book in the Library of Congress is *Old King Cole*. It is 1/25 of an inch (0.6 cm) by 1/25 of an inch (0.6 cm). The pages can only be turned with the use of a needle.

- There are over 375 organisations around the world devoted to Sherlock Holmes. The largest group is the Japan Sherlock Holmes Club, with over 1,200 members.

- The largest book in the Library of Congress is John James Audubon's *Birds of America*, containing life-size illustrations of birds. The book is 39.37 inches (1 m) high.

- 'Absterse' is a little-used verb meaning 'to clean'.

- Dr Seuss wrote *Green Eggs and Ham* after his editor dared him to write a book using fewer than 50 different words.

- The first issue of *Life* magazine – dated 23 November 1936 and featuring the work of photographer Margaret Bourke-White – sold for 10 cents.

──────── LANGUAGE AND LITERATURE ────────

- In 1955, a book was returned to Cambridge University Library – 288 years overdue.

- Victor Hugo was inspired to write *The Hunchback of Notre Dame* following a visit to Notre Dame Cathedral, where he discovered a cryptic inscription – the Greek word for 'fate' carved deep into a stone wall in the tower. As he pondered the origins and meaning of the message, a story began to take shape in his mind.

- American poet Emily Dickinson wrote more than 900 poems, of which only four were published during her lifetime.

- Robert Louis Stevenson said he had envisioned the entire story of *Dr Jekyll and Mr Hyde* in a dream and simply recorded it the way he saw it. Stevenson claimed to be able to dream plots for his stories at will.

- The Dr Seuss book *Yertle the Turtle* was based on Adolf Hitler, while *Marvin K. Mooney, Will You Please Go Away Now?* featured a character that is constantly asked to go away. The character was based on former president Richard M Nixon.

- *Gone with the Wind* was the only book written by Margaret Mitchell.

------- **LANGUAGE AND LITERATURE** -------

● Rudyard Kipling would only write when he had black ink in his pen.

● In America, *The Diary of Anne Frank* has been banned due to being too depressing for children.

● Shakespeare invented the phrase 'laugh it off' and the words 'bedroom' and 'puke'.

● Between 1986 and 1996, Brazilian author Jose Carlos Ryoki de Alpoim Inoue had 1,058 novels published.

● The first publication of the *Encyclopaedia Britannica* came out in 1768.

● Norwegian playwright Henrik Ibsen had a pet scorpion that he used to keep on his desk for inspiration.

● Barbara Bush's book about her English springer spaniel, *Millie's Book*, was on the best-seller list for 29 weeks. Millie was the most popular 'First Dog' in history.

● Charles Dickens always used to touch things three times for luck.

● Charles Dickens earned no more money from his many books than he did from doing lectures.

———— LANGUAGE AND LITERATURE ————

- Before he settled on the name Mark Twain, writer Samuel Clemens published work under the names Thomas Jefferson Snodgrass, Sergeant Fathom and W Apaminondas Adrastus Blab.

- Lewis Carroll wrote most of his books standing up.

- In the 1631 publication of the Bible, a printer accidentally omitted the word 'not' from the seventh commandment, encouraging readers to commit adultery.

- The very first book about plastic surgery was written in 1597.

- Russian writer Konstantin Mikhailov had 325 pseudonyms.

- Dr Samuel Johnson wrote the story *Rasselas* in one week so he could earn the money to pay for his mother's funeral.

- Lord Byron had an affair with his half-sister and made her pregnant.

- Ben Johnson had his heel bone stolen by the Dean of Westminster when his grave was disturbed in 1849. It later turned up again in a junk shop in 1938.

—— LANGUAGE AND LITERATURE ——

- Lord Alfred Tennyson once had a pony called Fanny, which used to pull his wife along in a wheelchair.

- Marcel Proust once had a pet swordfish.

- George Bernard Shaw was 29 years old when he lost his virginity to an elderly widow. This event traumatised him so much that he didn't have sex for another 15 years.

- D H Lawrence was a prude and would only make love in the dark.

- Hans Christian Andersen was so terrified of being killed in a fire that he always carried a piece of rope with him so that he could escape any building that was alight.

- During the Chinese Cultural Revolution, all literary works by Charles Dickens and William Shakespeare were banned.

- At one time, Chinese books had the footnotes printed at the top of the page.

- Samuel Pepys loved to play the recorder.

- Playwright Richard Brinsley Sheridan was such a compulsive drinker that he would drink eau de cologne.

——— LANGUAGE AND LITERATURE ———

- When the British painter and poet Rossetti's wife died, he decided to bury his book of poems with her. Seven years later, however, he changed his mind and decided that he wanted them back, so he arranged for the grave to be opened, removed the book of poems and had them disinfected. They were later published to great acclaim.

- In Shakespeare's *Julius Caesar* there is a reference to a clock striking, but clocks did not appear until at least a thousand years after Caesar's death.

- Dostoyevsky and F Scott Fitzgerald were both foot fetishists.

- John Milton received just £10 for *Paradise Lost* during his entire lifetime.

- American author Truman Capote would only ever write on yellow paper.

- William Prynne, the British pamphleteer, had his ears cut off because of his inflammatory publications.

- Anthony Trollope invented the pillarbox.

- Jane Austen's book *'Northanger Abbey* was originally called 'Susan'.

─────── **LANGUAGE AND LITERATURE** ───────

- William Ireland once forged a new version of *King Lear* and various other documents supposedly written by Shakespeare. He then wrote a story called *Voltigern*, which he claimed was a lost Shakespearean play. Many scholars examined the documents and declared them to be authentic, but when it was performed on stage it was so terrible that it was booed off.

- Charles Dickens would work himself up so much when he performed his own works on stage that he sometimes fainted.

- The *New York Times* once published an apology to a professor 49 years after his theories about travelling into space, which they had scoffed at, were proved to be correct.

- Winston Churchill wrote his book *The History of the English Speaking Peoples* when he was 82 years old.

- In Shakespeare's *The Winter's Tale*, he writes about a ship that has been wrecked off the coast of Bohemia, yet Bohemia has never had a coastline.

- Books that are made in the present day only have a life expectancy of about 100 years because the sulphuric acid in the wood-pulp paper rots rapidly.

———— **LANGUAGE AND LITERATURE** ————

- Robert Louis Stevenson was inspired by a real-life man, William Brodie, in the devising of his story *Dr Jekyll and Mr Hyde*. Brodie, a man who by day was a respected man of society and Deacon of Edinburgh, at night hung out in the lowest parts of the town, and murdered many people. He was hanged for his wrongdoings, but just beforehand he managed to slip a tube in his throat to prevent his neck from snapping. After the hanging, they cut him from the gallows and rushed him to his home, where a private doctor would try to revive him. When they opened his coffin, however, his corpse had disappeared.

- William Shakespeare's signature is worth millions of pounds, as there are only seven known specimens in the entire world.

- Ben Jonson was buried upright in Westminster Abbey's Poets' Corner because he died in debt and couldn't afford a proper gravesite.

- *Catch 22*, by Joseph Heller, was originally entitled 'Catch 18'.

- Robert Browning used Chianti to wean and cure his wife, Elizabeth Barrett Browning, from her addiction to laudanum.

———— LANGUAGE AND LITERATURE ————

- The first issue of *The Lady* magazine gave its readers detailed instructions on how to take a bath properly. In spite of being a woman's magazine, the article was illustrated with pictures of a man instead of a woman because of decency.

- There are more than 13,000 existing towns and cities in Great Britain that can claim to have been mentioned in the Domesday Book.

- Lord Byron, considered one of the most dashing and attractive men of his time, was overweight and had a club-foot.

- There is approximately one library book for each and every person on earth.

- After the death of her husband, poet Percy Shelley, Mary Shelley kept his heart wrapped up in silk until she died.

- Henrik Ibsen always had a picture of his arch-rival August Strindberg hanging over his desk so that it would make him work harder.

- In 1975, Indian poet Sri Chinmoy wrote 843 different poems in a single day.

———— LANGUAGE AND LITERATURE ————

- In Denmark, an author who wrote a book criticising the Swedes, who were at that time occupying his country, was arrested and then given the choice of either being beheaded or of eating his own words. He opted to eat his own words by boiling his book in broth and making a soup out of it.

- Charles Dickens' knowledge of Victorian life in London was mainly due to the fact that he would walk as much as 20 miles (32 km) a night around the streets of London to cure his insomnia.

- The very first newspaper to use a perfumed page was the *Washington Daily News*, in 1937.

- Lord Byron had four pet geese that he took everywhere with him, even to social gatherings.

- George Orwell worked as a policeman before turning to a writing career.

- More books have been written about Jack the Ripper than any other murderer in the world.

- Charles Darwin thought that the 1,250 first-run copies of his book *The Origin of Species* was too much, but they sold out the first day of publication.

——— LANGUAGE AND LITERATURE ———

- *The Great Gatsby* was originally entitled 'Incident at West Egg'.

- Edgar Rice Burroughs wrote 26 *Tarzan* books without ever visiting Africa.

- Beatrix Potter, famous for writing and illustrating the Peter Rabbit children's books, actually had a squirrel shot to death in order to provide a model for the character Nutkin, and had a rabbit killed with chloroform to provide the model for Peter Rabbit. When she needed a model for a fox character she had a recently killed fox skinned and boiled and the skeleton rebuilt.

- There is no living descendant of William Shakespeare.

- There have been copies made of the Holy Bible and the Koran that are small enough to fit in a walnut shell.

- In Turkey, during the 19th century, newspapers were severely censored, to such an extent that when the King and Queen of Turkey were murdered it was reported that they had both died of indigestion.

- Shelley hated cats so much that he once tied one to the string of a kite during a thunderstorm to see if it would be electrocuted.

———— # LANGUAGE AND LITERATURE ————

- Rudyard Kipling was fired as a reporter for the *San Francisco Examiner*. His dismissal letter said, 'I'm sorry, Mr Kipling, but you just don't know how to use the English language. This isn't a kindergarten for amateur writers.'

- John Grisham is a 16th cousin of President Bill Clinton.

- John Ruskin was so appalled by his wife's pubic hair on their wedding night that he totally gave up sex.

- In literature, the average length of a sentence is around 35 words.

- *Don Quixote* has been translated into more languages than any book apart from the Bible.

- It is believed that the Greek poet Aeschylus was killed when a bird flying overhead dropped a tortoise and struck him on the head. The bird had mistaken his bald head for a rock that would crack the tortoise's shell on impact.

- There really was a Cyrano de Bergerac. He lived from about 1620 to 1655, had a big nose and duelled. He was also a science-fiction writer who was the first person in history to suggest that a rocket could carry someone into space.

———— LANGUAGE AND LITERATURE ————

- James Joyce suffered from stomach ulcers most of his life and believed that the key to good health was defecation, and if he didn't get to do so at least three times a day he would fret. He was so fascinated by stools that he once asked his wife, Nora, to go on a piece of paper while he lay down underneath her and observed.

- Ernest Hemingway drove an ambulance during the World War I.

- After reading *Alice in Wonderland*, Queen Victoria sent a letter to author Lewis Carroll asking for another of his books to read. Carroll, who was also a brilliant mathematician, sent her a book on algebra.

- The young Charles Dickens wanted to be an actor.

- D H Lawrence enjoyed taking off his clothes and climbing mulberry trees.

- Emile Zola had two families with his wife and his mistress, and they all lived in the same house together.

- In the 17th century there once lived a real–life Victor Frankenstein. Physician Konrad Johann Dippel set up a laboratory at Frankenstein Castle, near Darmstat, Germany, where he could pursue his hobby of alchemy.

──────── **LANGUAGE AND LITERATURE** ────────

Like Victor Frankenstein of the novel, Dippel was also
interested in the possibility of immortality through
scientific means, and exhumed corpses from
Frankenstein's cemetery to experiment on. When the
town's people started to suspect him of stealing corpses,
he turned to trying the experiments on himself, and died
drinking one of these formulas.

● Leo Tolstoy's wife had to copy his manuscript of *War and
  Peace* by hand seven times.

● A Sunday edition of the *New York Times* uses the
  equivalent of 63,000 trees.

● Wilfred Owen's brother found himself inexplicably
  depressed amid a ship's celebrations at the end of the
  World War I. He went down to his cabin and saw Wilfred
  sitting in his chair with a characteristic expression that
  turned to a broad smile before he disappeared. The poet
  had been killed on the last day of the war.

15

ANIMALS

——— ANIMALS ———

- The ant always falls over to its right side when intoxicated.

- Starfish don't have brains.

- Turtles can breathe through their bottoms.

- Fish have no eyelids, as their eyes do not close.

- Seahorses are the only fish in which the head forms a right angle with the body.

- The pheasant originated in China.

- The arctic fox often follows the polar bear, feeding on the abandoned carcass of its kill.

- The stomach of a giraffe has four chambers.

- Baby squirrels are called kittens.

- A racoon appears to wash its food before eating it.

- The jaguar is the largest of the American big cats.

- The roadrunner is a member of the cuckoo family.

- The nesting site of penguins is called a rookery.

ANIMALS

- Desert-living gerbils never need to drink, as they obtain all the moisture they need from the overnight dew on their food.

- The elephant is the only mammal able to kneel on all fours.

- The feet of the puffin are red in summer and yellow in winter.

- Coyotes pair for life.

- A female walrus is called a cow.

- A male guinea pig is called a boar.

- The Falabella is the world's smallest breed of horse.

- Turkish van cats have a natural liking for water.

- A female mouse is called a doe.

- The dingo is the only carnivore native to Australia.

- In China the hedgehog is considered sacred.

- The Chinese crested dog is hairless.

ANIMALS

- Dolphins are the only species, barring humans, which have sex for pleasure.

- The anal glands of the African civet cat secrete a strong-smelling substance used in perfume manufacture.

- The part of a snail's body that remains inside the shell is called a mantle.

- The wolverine is sometimes known as the Glutton due to its enormous appetite.

- Lobsters are blue when alive and red when cooked.

- In ancient Canadian legend, the turtle was the oldest and wisest creature on earth before man came to the Americas.

16

FOOD

———————————— FOOD ————————————

- Laws forbidding the sale of fizzy drinks on Sunday prompted William Garwood to invent the ice-cream sundae in Illinois, in 1875.

- McDonald's and Burger King sugar-coat their fries so they will turn golden brown.

- The world's deadliest mushroom is the Amanita phalloides, the Death Cap. The five different poisons contained in the mushroom cause diarrhoea and vomiting within six to 12 hours of ingestion. This is followed by damage to the liver, kidneys and central nervous system – and finally, in the majority of cases, coma and death.

- In an authentic Chinese meal, the last course is soup because it allows the roast duck entrée to 'swim' towards digestion.

- When potatoes first appeared in Europe in the 17th century, it was thought that they were disgusting, and they were blamed for starting outbreaks of leprosy and syphilis. As late as 1720 in America, eating potatoes was believed to shorten a person's life.

- Since Hindus don't eat beef, the McDonald's in New Delhi makes its burgers with mutton.

FOOD

- Liquorice can raise your blood pressure.

- The largest item on any menu in the world is roast camel, sometimes served at Bedouin wedding feasts. The camel is stuffed with a sheep's carcass, which is stuffed with chickens, which are stuffed with fish, which are stuffed with eggs.

- The world's most expensive coffee, at $130 a pound, is called Kopi Luwak. It is in the droppings of a type of marsupial that eats only the very best coffee beans. Plantation workers track them and scoop their precious droppings.

- Large doses of coffee can be lethal. Ten grams, or 100 cups over four hours, can kill the average human.

- Lime Jell-o gives off the same brain waves as adult males.

- When Heinz ketchup leaves the bottle, it travels at a rate of 25 mph.

- A survey of international travellers revealed that the best restaurants in the world are in Paris. Second place was awarded to Rome, and third place went to Hong Kong.

- There are more than 30,000 diets on public record.

FOOD

- There are 18 different animal shapes in the Animal Crackers cookie zoo.

- A lion was the symbol for Dr Pepper's earliest ad campaign, used with the slogan 'King of Beverages'.

- From 1941 until 1950, violet was part of the colour mixture for M&M's plain chocolates, but was replaced by tan.

- The pumpkin has been known to develop roots whose total length reached 82,000 ft (24,994 m) – more than 15 miles (24 km).

- Chocolate manufacturers use 40% of the world's almonds and 20% of the world's peanuts.

- In 1938, a comic strip was used to advertise Pepsi-Cola. It was titled 'Pepsi and Pete'.

- Of about 350 million cans of chicken noodle soup, of all commercial brands, sold annually in the United States, 60% are purchased during the cold and flu season. January is the top-selling month of the year.

- Official guidelines allow whole pepper to be sold with up to 1% of the volume made up of rodent droppings.

FOOD

- Centuries ago, men were told that the evil effects of coffee would make them sterile; women were cautioned to avoid caffeine unless they wanted to be barren.

- 'Okonomiyaki' is considered to be Japan's answer to pizza. It consists of a pot-pourri of grilled vegetables, noodles, and meat or seafood, placed between two pancake-like layers of fried batter.

- In 1954, US food company General Mills introduced Trix breakfast cereal. The new cereal, a huge hit with kids, was 46.6% sugar.

- Olive oil is made only from green olives. Nearly the entire production of green olives grown in Italy is converted into olive oil.

- 'Colonial goose' is the name Australians give to stuffed mutton.

- 'Poached egg' means 'egg-in-a-bag' from the French word 'poche'. When an egg is poached, the white of the egg forms a pocket around the yolk, hence the name.

- In Alaska's Matanuska Valley, the long hours of sunlight are used by some farmers to grow giant vegetables. One such farmer grew a 100-lb (45 kg) cabbage.

FOOD

- 'Grunt' and 'slump' are two names that refer to a fruit dessert with a biscuit topping.

- 'Sherbet' is Australian slang for beer.

- 'Baby-cut' carrots aren't baby carrots. They're actually full-sized ones peeled and ground down to size.

- The US magazine *Cook's Illustrated* conducted blind-taste testings of vanillas, and the staff was surprised to find that, in baked goods, expensive, aromatic vanillas performed almost exactly the same as the cheaper brands of real vanilla. The differences virtually disappeared during cooking.

- On the Italian Riviera in Viareggio, there is a culinary tradition that a good soup must always contain one stone from the sea. This stems from the days when an Italian fisherman's catch was scooped up in nets; fish and stones frequently ended up together in the same cooking pot.

- In 1996, US company Gerber introduced Chicken Alfredo as one of its new flavours of baby food.

- In a traditional French restaurant kitchen, a *Garde Manger* is the person responsible for the preparation of cold foods.

FOOD

- In ancient China and certain parts of India, mouse flesh was considered a great delicacy.

- Once an orange is squeezed or cut, the vitamin C dissipates quickly. After only eight hours at room temperature or a scant 24 hours in the refrigerator, there is a 20% vitamin C loss.

- You would have to eat 11 lb (5 kg) of potatoes to put on 1 lb (0.45 kg) of weight – a potato has no more calories than an apple.

- One of the fattiest fishes is salmon: 4 oz (about 112 g) of the delectable fish contains 9 g of fat.

- Oysters were a major part of life in New York in the late 1800s. They were eaten for breakfast, lunch and dinner; they were pickled, stewed, baked, roasted, fried, scalloped and used in soups, patties and puddings. Oystering in New York supported large numbers of families, and oyster theft was a prevalent problem.

- One tablespoon of most brands of ketchup contains 4 g of sugar, 15 calories and 190 g of sodium. There is no fat in ketchup and processed red tomatoes are supposed to be a good source of lycopene, which may reduce the risk of cancer and other diseases.

FOOD

- In ancient Greece, where the mouse was sacred to Apollo, mice were sometimes devoured by temple priests.

- The chocolate-and-hazelnut spread Nutella is virtually unknown in America.

- The custom of serving a slice of lemon with fish dates back to the Middle Ages. It was believed that if a person accidentally swallowed a fish bone, the lemon juice would dissolve it.

- The darker the olive, the higher the oil content.

- The dessert parfait's name comes from the French word for 'perfect'.

- The drink Ovaltine was originally named 'Ovomaltine', but a clerical error changed it when the manufacturer registered the name.

- Only men were allowed to eat at the first self-service restaurant, The Exchange Buffet, in New York in 1885.

- Peanut oil is used for underwater cooking in submarines. Undersea fleets like it because it does not smoke unless heated above 450°F (232°C).

FOOD

- In ancient Rome, flamingo tongues were considered a great delicacy. Their existence was threatened by hunters, so the Romans made a law making it illegal to hunt flamingos, but it failed.

- In ancient Rome, it was considered a sin to eat the flesh of a woodpecker.

- In ancient Rome, oysters were so highly prized that they were sold for their weight in gold.

- The early American Indians of south-western United States only ate the organs of the animals they hunted for food, and left the muscles for predatory animals. Their meat-eating habits were changed by European influences.

- The ancient Greeks considered parsley too sacred to eat, while Romans served it as a garnish and to improve the taste of food. They believed it had special powers and would keep them sober.

- Peas will lose their bright green colour if cooked in a covered pot with acidic ingredients, such as lemon juice, wine, or tomatoes.

- Paper can be made from asparagus.

———————————— FOOD ————————————

- In the Middle East, and later in Europe, doctors blamed the aubergine for all sorts of things, from epilepsy to cancer. In the fifth century, Chinese women made a black dye from the aubergine skins to stain and polish their teeth, while some people in medieval Europe considered it an aphrodisiac.

- The Egyptians ate mustard by tossing the seeds into their mouths while chewing meat.

- Pears ripen better off the tree, and they ripen from the inside out.

- The first bottles of Coca-Cola sold for a mere three pence per bottle in 1899.

- Pecan crops need a freeze to help loosen the nuts from their shells.

- In ancient times, parsley wreaths were used to ward off drunkenness.

- In the Middle Ages, sugar was a treasured luxury, costing nine times as much as milk.

- The can opener was invented 48 years after cans were introduced.

FOOD

- The first beer brewed in England was made by the Picts in about 250 BC. The beverage was made from heather and may have had hallucinogenic properties.

- In early 1999, General Mills launched an 'Around the World Event' promotion with internationally known marshmallow shapes in its Lucky Charms cereal. These shapes included a purple Liberty Bell, a pink-and-white Leaning Tower of Pisa, a green-and-yellow torch, a gold pyramid, a blue Eiffel Tower, an orange Golden Gate Bridge, a green-and-white Alps, and a red-and-white Big Ben clock.

- The first-known pizza shop, Port Alba in Naples, opened in 1830 and is still open today.

- The average chocolate bar has 8 insects' legs in it.

- About 27% of food in developed countries is wasted each year, being simply thrown away.

- An onion, apple and potato all have the same taste. The differences in flavour are caused by their smell.

- With two forks and a charge, a pickle will emit light.

- Tibetans drink tea made of salt and rancid yak butter.

---------------------------------- FOOD ----------------------------------

- Nachos are the food most craved by American mothers-to-be.

- The average French citizen eats 500 snails a year.

- One pound (0.45 kg) of tea can make nearly 300 cups to drink.

- In the Middle Ages, chicken soup was believed to be an aphrodisiac.

- Bananas are consistently the number-one complaint of grocery shoppers. Most people complain when bananas are overripe or even freckled. The fact is that spotted bananas are sweeter, with a sugar content of more than 20%, compared with 3% in a green banana.

- Milk is considered to be a food and not a beverage.

- The cashew nut, in its natural state, contains poisonous oil. Roasting removes the oil and makes the nuts safe to eat.

- The strawberry is the only agricultural product that bears its seeds on the outside.

- Cheese is the oldest of all man-made foods.

FOOD

- The white part of an egg is called the 'glair'.

- There is more alcohol in mouthwash than in wine.

- Four per cent of the food you eat will be eaten in front of a refrigerator with its door open.

- Tomatoes with a strawberry inside have been successfully grown.

- There is a wild edible plant called Hernandulcin that is a thousand times sweeter than sugar.

- The boysenberry is a mixture of the blackberry, loganberry and raspberry.

- The carob can be used to replace chocolate in cooking.

- The word 'whisky' comes from the Gaelic *uisge beatha*, meaning 'water of life'.

- The globe artichoke belongs to the daisy family.

- The turnip originated in Greece.

- Grasshoppers are the most popular insect snack in some parts of the world.

FOOD

- Corn is the only cereal crop with American origins.

- Kohlrabi is a cross between a cabbage and a turnip.

- Tea-bags were first launched in the 1920s.

- One in five chickens in the supermarket are infected with *Campylobacter*, a bacterium that can cause food poisoning.

17

AMERICA AND AMERICANS

——— AMERICA AND AMERICANS ———

- Bacteria, including staphylococcus, E. coli, and Klebsiella, are present on 18% of the coins and 7% of the bills in the US.

- One in five Native Americans die in accidents, compared with 1 in 17 of the general American population.

- During the peak of its construction, the building of the Empire State Building proceeded at a pace of four-and-a-half storeys per week.

- A survey of 18- to 24-year-olds from nine nations put the United States last in general geographic knowledge scores. One in seven – about 24 million people – could not find their own country on a world map. And even more alarming, those who participated in the survey were recent high school and college graduates.

- Bat Cave, Duck, Horneytown, Whynot, Welcome, Toast and Frog Pond are all places in the state of North Carolina.

- In the US, more than 50% of the people who are bitten by venomous snakes, and go untreated, still survive.

- Louisiana is home to places such as Uncle Sam, Waterproof, Dry Prong and Belcher.

———— **AMERICA AND AMERICANS** ————

● Due to the Great Depression, it took over 12 years to occupy all the office space in the Empire State Building, earning it the nickname the 'Empty State Building'.

● The average American makes six trips to the bathroom every day.

● Ronald Reagan was the oldest man elected president.

● Until there was a pay rise in 1814, US congressmen were paid $6 per diem when Congress was in session.

● Prior to the adoption of the Twelfth Amendment in 1804, the candidate who ran second in a presidential race automatically became vice-president. Thomas Jefferson became John Adams's vice-president in this way.

● The American settlers took six months to reach the west coast by wagon between 1840 and 1850.

● Cut and planed lumber was hard to come by in the New World, and since the Pilgrims didn't intend to return to Europe, they dismantled the Mayflower and used its lumber to build a barn.

● Residents of Nevada bet an average of £475 a year in gambling casinos.

AMERICA AND AMERICANS

- By the end of the US Civil War, between one-third and one-half of all US paper currency in circulation was counterfeit, and so the US Secret Service was created under the US Treasury Department. In less than a decade, counterfeiting was sharply reduced.

- The official state musical instrument in South Dakota is the fiddle.

- Nearly a quarter of all United States pet owners take their pets to work.

- In June 2003, 200 American companies participated in the first ever 'Take Your Dog to Work Day'.

- In 1791, Washington DC was known as Federal City.

- The official state cooking pot of Utah is the Dutch oven.

- During the American Revolution, inflation was so great that the price of corn rose 10,000%, the price of wheat 14,000%, the price of flour 15,000%, and the price of beef 33,000%.

- Ronald Reagan was the first president to submit a trillion dollar budget to Congress.

AMERICA AND AMERICANS

- Twenty-five per cent of Americans do not know what is meant by the term 'holocaust'.

- The roadrunner is the official bird of New Mexico.

- It is illegal for kids to buy lollipops in Spokane, Washington.

- Approximately 40% of Americans believe they have food allergies, while in reality, less than 1% has true allergies. Most of the others involve symptoms caused by food intolerances or other disorders.

- The second National City is Port Angeles, Washington, designated by President Abraham Lincoln. That's where they would move the capital if something happened to Washington DC.

- During the 13-14 July 1977 black-out in New York City, a record 80 million telephone calls were made.

- Sixty-two per cent of American dog owners sign letters or cards from themselves and their dogs.

- The state of Maine has at least 28 cities or towns that begin with the word 'North', 23 with the word 'South', 22 with 'West', and 28 with 'East'.

—————— AMERICA AND AMERICANS ——————

- The state motto of Washington is 'Alki', Chinook Indian for 'By and By'.

- During World War II, the US Navy commissioned the world's first floating ice-cream parlour for service in the Pacific theatre. This concrete barge, capable of producing 10 gallons (38 litres) of ice-cream every seven seconds, kept ships well supplied.

- There are places called Boring, Cockeysville, Accident, Secretary and Assawoman Bay in the state of Maryland.

- The state of Pennsylvania can lay claim to the first woman governor, the first zip fastener, the first use of toilet paper and the autogiro, the ancestor to the helicopter.

- Phone calls in the United States plummeted as much as 58% during the reading of the O J Simpson trial verdict in 1995, as workers put their jobs on hold for up to 30 minutes. In contrast, phone-call volume barely budged when President John F Kennedy was assassinated.

- Sculptor Gutzon Borglum spent 14 years sculpting the busts of Presidents George Washington, Thomas Jefferson, Theodore Roosevelt and Abraham Lincoln on Mount Rushmore. When he died, his son continued his work.

———— AMERICA AND AMERICANS ————

- In the US there are about 15,000 people in comas.

- The state of Maine was once known as the 'Earmuff Capital of The World' as earmuffs were invented there by Chester Greenwood in 1873.

- President Richard Nixon visited both China and the Soviet Union during his term. He was also the first president to visit all 50 states.

- The US Automobile Association was formed in 1905 for the purpose or providing 'scouts' who could warn motorists of hidden police traps.

- There are three million stutterers in the United States and a similar proportion in every other part of the world.

- There are places called Conception, Peculiar, Frankenstein, Tightwad, Humansville and Enough in Missouri.

- The state of Oregon has one city named Sisters and another called Brothers. Sisters got its name from a nearby trio of peaks in the Cascade Mountains known as the Three Sisters. Brothers was named as a counterpart to Sisters.

—— AMERICA AND AMERICANS ——

- The Declaration of Independence is currently housed in the National Archives, and at one point it was actually repaired with Scotch tape.

- Textbook shortages are so severe in some US public schools that 71% of teachers say they have purchased reading materials with their own money.

- In 1933, a night's stay in a double room at the famous Waldorf-Astoria Hotel in New York City was £10. A single room cost £3.30 and a suite £10.20.

- The state of Minnesota is home to Embarrass, Fertile, Nowthen, Savage and Sleepy Eye.

- Wyoming was the first American state to allow women to vote.

- Forty-nine per cent of Americans don't know that white bread is made from wheat.

- New York City is the sister city of Tokyo.

- There was once an Anti-Tipping Society of America.

- It is illegal to wipe dishes dry in Minneapolis, Minnesota. Dishes should be left to drip dry.

——— AMERICA AND AMERICANS ———

- When Franklin D Roosevelt died on 12 April 1945, Harry Truman became the first US president to take office in the midst of a war.

- More than 40% of the women in the United States were in the Girl Scouts organisation. Two-thirds of the women listed in *Who's Who of Women* were Girl Scouts.

- The states of Arizona, Indiana and Hawaii have never adopted Daylight Savings Time. Neither has Puerto Rico, the Virgin Islands or American Samoa.

- Crummies, Dwarf, Monkey's Eyebrow, Rabbit Hash, Ordinary, Possum Trot, Oddville, Mud Lick, Hand Shoe and Bugtussle are all places in Kentucky.

- FBI agents were first allowed to carry guns in 1934, 26 years after the agency was established.

- The streets of Victor, Colorado, once a gold-rush town, are paved with low-grade gold.

- The average American's diet today consists of 55% junk food.

- When Andrew Johnson, the first US president to be impeached, died, he asked to be wrapped in an American

———— **AMERICA AND AMERICANS** ————

flag with a copy of the Constitution under his head when he was buried.

- Thirty-three per cent of American dog owners admit that they talk to their dogs on the phone or leave messages on an answering machine while away.

- The Hoover Dam is 726 ft (221 m) tall and 660 ft (201 m) thick at its base. Enough rock was excavated in its construction to build the Great Wall of China.

- The town of Fort Atkinson, Iowa, was the site of the only fort ever built by the US government to protect one Indian tribe from another.

- The United States consumes 50% of the world's production of diamonds. However, there is only one diamond mine located in the United States – in Arkansas.

- When he saw his assassin being beaten by his guards, the dying President William McKinley cried out, 'Don't let them hurt him.'

- Philadelphia is a city of big tippers: 18.6% of the bill minus tax is the normal amount given. Second place in the tip wars goes to New York City, with 18.3%. The

———— AMERICA AND AMERICANS ————

lowest tipping city in America is Seattle, where the average tip is 17.1%.

- Worms, Colon and Surprise are to be found in the state of Nebraska.

- American teenagers bet as much as $1 billion a year, and about 7% of adolescents under 18 may be addicted to gambling.

- Eight per cent of American kissers keep their eyes open, while more than 20% take an occasional peek.

- While serving as a young naval officer in World War II, President Richard M Nixon set up the only hamburger stand in the South Pacific. Nixon's Snack Shack served free burgers and Australian beer to flight crews.

- The Pentagon, in Arlington, Virginia, has twice as many bathrooms as is necessary. When it was built in the 1940s, the state of Virginia still had segregation laws requiring separate toilet facilities for blacks and whites.

- Since 1874, the mints of the United States have been making currency for foreign governments, whose combined orders have at times exceeded the volume of domestic requirements.

──────── **AMERICA AND AMERICANS** ────────

- The United States today contains more than 100,000 mounds, earthworks and fortifications that were built thousands of years ago by prehistoric races.

- Trident-missile manufacturer Lockheed transmits data from its Sunnyvale, California, headquarters to its Santa Cruz plant 30 miles (48 km) away via carrier pigeon.

- Twenty-one per cent of American children eat chocolate every day.

- Almost 90% of Americans label themselves as shy.

- The world's shortest river – the D River in Oregon – is only 121 ft (37 m) long.

- There are places called Manly, Gravity, Diagonal and What Cheer in the state of Iowa.

- A study of New York marathoners a few years ago found that their divorce rate – male and female – was twice the national average.

- Persons that engage in solitary endurance sports are the ones most likely to be compulsive exercisers – for example, joggers, long-distance swimmers, weight lifters, and cross-country skiers. Occasionally, devotees of these

—————— AMERICA AND AMERICANS ——————

activities set unrealistic, ambitious goals and then drive themselves mercilessly to reach them.

● Although the United States has just 5% of the world's population, it has most of the world's lawyers, at 70%.

● The world's largest Yo-Yo resides in the National Yo-yo Museum in Chico, California. Named 'Big Yo', it is 256 lb (116 kg), 50 inches (127 cm) tall and 31.5 inches (80 cm) wide.

● President Richard M Nixon suffered from motion sickness and hay fever.

● The United States would fit into the continent of Africa three and a half times.

● Odd place names in Maine include Bald Head, Robinhood and Beans Corner Bingo.

● There are 61 towns in the United States with the word 'turkey' in their names – for example, Turkeytown, Alabama, and Turkey Foot, Florida.

● President Abraham Lincoln considered his Gettysburg Address 'a flat failure'.

—— AMERICA AND AMERICANS ——

● There are 40 active volcanoes in Alaska – more than in any other US state.

● There are 293 ways to make change for a dollar.

● Americans consume about 138 billion cups of coffee a year.

● You can fold a piece of US currency forward then backward about 4,000 times before it will tear.

● It is illegal to ride a bike into a swimming pool in Baldwin Park, California.

● Americans today consume nearly the same number of calories per day as Americans did in 1910, but the weight of the average American has increased substantially due to lack of exercise.

● Americans pay over $30,000 in federal, state and local taxes every second.

● Using satellite-surveying techniques, scientists have determined that Los Angeles, California, is moving east. At a rate estimated to be about one-fifth of an inch (0.5 cm) per year, the city is moving closer to the San Gabriel Mountains.

AMERICA AND AMERICANS

- One million dollars in $1 bills would weigh approximately one ton. Placed in a pile, the pile would be 360 feet (110 metres) high — as tall as 60 average adults standing on top of each other.

- There are more than 100,000 glaciers in Alaska, and about 75% of all the fresh water in the state is stored as glacial ice.

- In 1980, the Yellow Pages accidentally listed a Texas funeral home under Frozen Foods.

- 'Uncle Jumbo' was the nickname of President Grover Cleveland.

- There are places called French Lick, Gnaw Bone, Fickle, Plainville, Gas City and Floyd's Knobs in Indiana.

- Americans today, per capita, use four times as much energy as their grandparents' generation did.

- The 10 most popular girl's names in America are Emily, Madison, Hannah, Emma, Alexis, Ashley, Abigail, Sarah, Samantha and Olivia.

- The state of West Virginia is home to Crum, War, Pinch, Big Ugly, Left Hand and Lost City.

AMERICA AND AMERICANS

- The United States had a Society for the Prevention of Cruelty to Animals in 1866, eight years before it had a Society for the Prevention of Cruelty to Children.

- Utah is known as the 'Beehive State'.

- Americans use 50 million tons of paper a year.

- Alaska was bought from Russia for about 2 cents an acre.

- Americans will hold more parties in their homes on Super Bowl Sunday than any other day of the year.

- Various US cities are named after other countries. You can visit the US city of Peru in the states of Maine, Nebraska and New York.

- About 24% of American adults say they have participated, at some time or another, in illegal gambling.

- There are about 3,000 hot-dog vendors in metropolitan New York.

- There are four places in the United States with the word 'chicken' in their name: Chicken, Alaska; Chicken Bristle, in Illinois and Kentucky; and Chickentown, Pennsylvania.

AMERICA AND AMERICANS

- Mail to the Havasupai Indian Reservation, in northern Arizona, is delivered by mule. It is the only US Postal Service route of its type in existence today.

- About 60% of all American babies are named after close relatives.

- There is one slot machine in Las Vegas for every eight inhabitants.

- President Richard M Nixon kept a music box in his Oval Office desk that played the tune 'Hail to the Chief'.

- About 70% of American households buy yellow mustard every year.

- Richard M Nixon is the only president to have resigned.

- There are over three million lakes in Alaska. The largest, Lake Iliamna, is the size of Connecticut.

- Washington boasts places called Forks, Index and Tumtum.

- An estimated one in five Americans — some 38 million — don't like sex.

AMERICA AND AMERICANS

- Twelve million Americans do not know that their nation's capital is Washington DC.

- Unlike other US presidents, Jimmy Carter avoided using his initials because 'JC' is usually associated with Jesus Christ.

- It is illegal for dogs to get in the way of people walking in Pateros, Washington.

- Green Bay, Wisconsin, lays claim to being 'The Toilet Paper Capital of The World'. Some other notable Wisconsin capitals include: Belleville – UFO Capital of Wisconsin; Bloomer – Jump Rope Capital of the World; Bonduel – Spelling Capital of Wisconsin; Boscobel – Turkey Capital of Wisconsin; Hayward – Muskie Capital of the World; Mercer – Loon Capital of the World; Monroe – Swiss Cheese Capital of the World; Mount Horeb – Troll Capital of the World; Muscoda – Morel Mushroom Capital of Wisconsin; Potosi – Catfish Capital of Wisconsin; Sheboygan – Bratwurst Capital of the World; Somerset – Inner Tubing Capital of the World; Sturgeon Bay – Shipbuilding Capital of the Great Lakes; and Wausau – Ginseng Capital of the World.

- The state of California has issued six driver's licences to Jesus Christ.

────────── **AMERICA AND AMERICANS** ──────────

● Odd place names in Illinois include Roachtown, Fishhook, Grand Detour, Kickapoo, Normal and Oblong.

● Various US cities have been named after popular European cities. For example, Paris could mean the city located in any of the states of Arkansas, Florida, Idaho, Illinois, Kentucky, Massachusetts, Tennessee, Texas or West Virginia.

● The largest of the 130 national cemeteries in America is the Calverton National Cemetery, on Long Island, New York. It conducts more than 7,000 burials each year.

● More than 2.2 million guests visited Dollywood, Dolly Parton's theme park, in 1998, making the park the most visited attraction in the state of Tennessee after the Great Smoky Mountains National Park. //include in arts section?//

● Twenty per cent of Americans don't know that Osama Bin Laden and Saddam Hussein are different people.

● Virginia extends 95 miles (153 km) further west than West Virginia.

● Presidents George Washington and John Adams had to

AMERICA AND AMERICANS

employ protection money, paying off certain pirates in the Mediterranean Sea with a couple of million dollars, while Congress debated the creation of a US navy.

- Texas is home to locations such as Bacon, Looneyville, Wink, Oatmeal and Noodle.

- More than 40% of American households with children have guns.

- Montpelier, Vermont, is the only US state capital without a McDonald's.

- More than 80 languages are spoken in New York. The second most common language spoken, after English, is Spanish.

- The city morgue in the Bronx, New York, has been so busy at times that next of kin take numbers and wait in line for their body-identification call.

- In America, 175,000 new laws and two million new regulations are introduced every year, from all levels of government.

- In the United States, courts of law devote about half their time to cases involving cars.

—— AMERICA AND AMERICANS ——

- Four states have active volcanoes: Washington, California, Alaska and Hawaii, with the latter being home to Mauna Loa, the world's largest active volcano. Hawaii itself was formed by the activity of undersea volcanoes.

- In the United States there are two credit cards for every person.

- New York City, named by Americans as the most dangerous, least attractive and rudest city, is also Americans' top choice as the city where they would most like to live or visit on vacation.

- Abraham Lincoln was the first president born outside the original 13 colonies.

- Mount Carmel is one of Chicago's finest graveyards, and is most famous for the graves of Chicago's notorious gangsters of the 1920s – including the infamous Al Capone.

- Georgia boasts places called Cumming, Hopeulikit and Between.

- The United States produces 19% of the world's trash. The annual contribution includes 20 billion disposable nappies and two billion razors.

—— AMERICA AND AMERICANS ——

- The United States earned the title of having the most cars of any country in the world. With an estimated 135 million cars nation-wide, it is approximated that there is one car for every two Americans.

- It is illegal to enter a public theatre or a tram within four hours of eating garlic in Gary, Indiana.

- There are more Irish in New York City than in Dublin, more Italians in New York City than in Rome, Italy; and more Jews in New York City than in Tel Aviv, Israel.

- Ulysses S Grant was the first president whose parents were both alive when he was inaugurated.

- Myrtle Beach, South Carolina, has the most mini-golf courses per area in the United States.

- In the United States most car journeys are less than 5 miles (8 km).

- In the United States the most popular colour for textiles is blue, though blue is one of the least-favourite colours for house paint.

- From the 1830s to 1960s, the Lehigh River, in eastern Pennsylvania, was owned by the Lehigh Coal and

AMERICA AND AMERICANS

Navigation Company, making it the only privately owned river in the United States.

- The United States shreds 7,000 tons (7,112,000 kg) of worn-out currency each year.

- The state of Tennessee boasts locations called Defeated, Static, Nameless, Disco, Difficult, Finger and Life.

- William Henry Harrison was the first US president to die while in office. He also had the shortest term in office (32 days), falling ill with pneumonia shortly after his inauguration and never recovering.

- In the United States, it is estimated that four million 'junk' telephone calls – phone solicitations by persons or programmed machine – are made every day.

- Grasshopper Glacier, in Montana, was named for the grasshoppers that can still be seen frozen in the ice.

- The average North American will eat 35,000 cookies during their life span.

- Before the enactment of the 1978 law that made it mandatory for dog owners in New York City to clean up after their pets, approximately 40 million pounds (around

AMERICA AND AMERICANS

18 million kilograms) of dog excrement were deposited on the streets every year.

- There are more people in New York City (7.9 million) than there are in the states of Alaska, Vermont, Wyoming, South Dakota, New Hampshire, Nevada, Idaho, Utah, Hawaii, Delaware and New Mexico combined.

- In the US, the penny and the Sacagawea dollar are the only coins currently minted with profiles that face to the right. All other US coins – the half dollar, quarter, dime, and nickel – feature profiles that face to the left.

- Bad Axe, Eden, Jugville, Hell, Pigeon and Paradise are all places found in the state of Michigan.

- Hawaii's 'Forbidden Island' of Nihau is owned by a single family named Robinson. On Nihau, there are no phones and no electricity for the population of 250 Hawaiians living there.

- The American Mint once considered producing doughnut-shaped coins.

- At some US malls, security patrols use horses to increase car park security, but at times report a 'Code Brown', meaning one of the horses has made a mess.

AMERICA AND AMERICANS

- Christmas, Frostproof, Niceville, Two Egg and Yellow Water are places in Florida.

- President George Washington was the first person to breed roses in the US. He laid out his own garden at Mount Vernon and filled it with his own selections of roses. One of the varieties was named after his mother and it is still being grown today.

- Hawaii has 150 recognised ecosystems.

- There are more telephones than people in Washington DC.

- There are more television sets in the United States than there are people in Japan.

- President Bill Clinton is allergic to dust, mould, pollen, cats, Christmas trees and dairy products.

- President Rutherford B Hayes' wife, Lucy Webb, was the initial First Lady to graduate from college and did not allow drinking in the White House, earning her the nickname 'Lemonade Lucy'.

- Wall, Farmer, Oral, Potato Creek, Igloo and Hammer are all places in the state of South Dakota.

AMERICA AND AMERICANS

- Almost a quarter of the land area of Los Angeles is taken up by cars.

- So confident were some people that alcohol was the cause of virtually all crime that, on the eve of Prohibition, some US towns actually sold their jails.

- It is illegal to push dirt under a rug in Pittsburgh, Pennsylvania.

- There are more art galleries in Scottsdale, Arizona, than either Los Angeles or San Francisco.

- President William Taft was the last president to keep a cow on the White House lawn to supply him with fresh milk.

- Hell's Canyon, on the Snake River in Idaho, is deeper than the Grand Canyon.

- The two most commonly sold items in American grocery stores are breakfast cereals and fizzy drink.

- The state of North Dakota boasts locations called Colgate, Zap, Antler, Concrete and Hoople.

- The Capitol Records building in Los Angeles, California, is built to resemble a stack of records. A red plane-

AMERICA AND AMERICANS

warning light atop the structure flashes out the word 'Hollywood' in Morse code every 20 seconds.

- Reno, Nevada, has the highest rate of alcoholism in the United States; Provo, Utah, has the lowest rate.

- In terms of resources used and pollution contributed in a lifetime, one citizen of the United States is the equivalent of about 80 citizens of India.

- If the Nile River were stretched across the United States, it would run just about from New York to Los Angeles.

- A shot of Elvis Presley offering his services as a drug enforcement agent to Nixon is the most requested photo from the US National Archives.

- The state of New Hampshire is home to Hell Hollow, Lost Nation and Sandwich Landing.

- Technically, there are really only 46 states in the United States, as Kentucky, Massachusetts, Pennsylvania and Virginia are commonwealths.

- The 10 most popular boys' names in America are Jacob, Michael, Joshua, Matthew, Ethan, Joseph, Andrew, Christopher, Daniel and Nicholas.

——————— AMERICA AND AMERICANS ———————

- The Alaskan island of Little Diomede is only 2 1/2 miles (4 km) away from the Russian coast.

- Fifty-two per cent of Americans think early man coexisted with the dinosaurs.

- There are places in Colorado called Climax, No Name, Hygiene, Dinosaur and Last Chance.

- In the United States, 25,300,500 out of more than 40 million dogs can perform at least one trick: 5,313,105 dogs can sit, 3,795,075 can shake paws, and 379,508 dogs can 'say prayers'.

- The Capitol Building in Washington DC has 365 steps. They represent the days of the year.

- President William McKinley had a pet parrot that he named 'Washington Post'.

- In 1995, KFC sold 11 pieces of chicken for every man, woman and child in the US.

- Located in Cochise County, in southern Arizona, the city of Tombstone is probably the most famous and most glamorised mining town in all of North America. According to legend, prospectors Ed Schieffelin and his

--------- **AMERICA AND AMERICANS** ---------

brother Al were warned not to venture into the Apache-inhabited Mule Mountains because they would only 'find their tombstones'. Thus, with a touch of the macabre, the Schieffelins named their first silver strike claim Tombstone, and it became the name of the town.

- Two towns in Vermont claim to be President Chester Arthur's birthplace, but recent research supports his opponents' charges that he was born in Canada, and therefore was not eligible to be president under the US Constitution.

- Maine is the only US state that adjoins only one other state.

- Abraham Lincoln was the first US president to leave no will.

- In the United States, deaf people have safer driving records than hearing people.

- On 10 July 1913, Death Valley had the hottest temperature recorded in the western hemisphere when, in the shade, it reached 134°F (56.6°C).

- In the United States, the number of women living alone has risen 33% to 30 million in the past 15 years.

--------- **AMERICA AND AMERICANS** ---------

- Colorado's capital of Denver is the largest metro city in a 600-mile radius (966 km) – an area almost the size of Europe.

- Bumpass, Nuttsville, Kermit, Cuckoo, Ben Hur, Threeway and Pocket can all be found in the state of Virginia.

- There is only one city in the United States named merely 'Beach'. It is found in North Dakota, which is a land-locked state.

- It is illegal for a barber to shave a customer's chest in Omaha, Nebraska.

- There are places in the state of Montana called Square Butt, Hungry Horse, Divide and Rocky Boy.

- Meadowcroft Rock Shelter, in Washington County, Pennsylvania, is the earliest documented place of human habitation in the western hemisphere. Studies done by anthropologist Dr James Adovasio found evidence of early civilisations. Carbon dating revealed the remains were from human habitants living in the area 16,240 years ago.

- Seventy-five per cent of all American women wear a bra that is the wrong size.

—— AMERICA AND AMERICANS ——

- There are locations in Vermont called Satan's Kingdom, Mosquitoville and Notown.

- At the height of the Great Depression in 1932, 12 million people in the US were unemployed.

- Out of the 34,000 gun deaths in the United States each year, fewer than 300 are listed as 'justifiable homicide', the only category that could include shooting a burglar, mugger, or rapist.

- There are places called Wimp, Sucker Flat, Squabbletown, Rough and Ready, Bummerville and Frying Pan in California.

- The New York Stock Exchange had its first million-share trading day in 1886.

- About 66% of magazines found tossed along US roadsides are pornographic.

- After telling the press he was an expert in hand gestures, President George Bush gave the 'V for Victory' sign as he drove past demonstrators in Canberra, Australia. In Australia, holding up two fingers to form a 'V' has the same vulgar meaning as the middle-finger gesture in Britain. The demonstrators were enraged, and they

——— AMERICA AND AMERICANS ———

signalled in the same manner back at the US President, who later apologised for his *faux pas*.

- Odd place names in Oregon include Idiotville, Windmaster Corner, Drain and Boring.

- More than 100,000 Americans die annually from adverse reactions to prescription drugs.

- At any given time during the day, there is an average of 150,000 people airborne over the United States.
- Michigan was the first US state to have roadside picnic tables.

- Occasionally, hot-dog sales at baseball stadiums exceed attendance, but typically hot-dog sales at ballparks average 80% of the attendance.

- More than one in nine cars in the United States will be in a collision in any given year.

- There are places called Elephant Butte, Tingle, Truth or Consequences and Texico in New Mexico.

- Potato chips are Americans' favourite snack food. They are devoured at a rate of 1.2 billion pounds (around 540 million kilograms) a year.

AMERICA AND AMERICANS

● President William McKinley always wore a red carnation in his lapel for good luck.

● Each tour through Natural Bridge Caverns in Texas covers 3/4 mile (1.2 km). An average tour guide will walk almost 560 miles (901 km) in one year while on the job.

● Broadway contains 35 theatres with the capacity to seat a combined 42,000 people.

● The state of Oklahoma contains places called Slaughterville, Okay, Cookietown, Happy Land and Bowlegs.

● The population of the American colonies in 1610 was 350.

● Forty-nine per cent of American fathers describe themselves as better parents than their dads.

● There are places in the state of Kansas called Ransom, Buttermilk and Admire.

● With 20.7 divorces out of every 1,000 married people, the United States leads the world in broken marriages. The closest 'rival' is Denmark, with 13.1 divorces per 1,000 marriages.

—————— AMERICA AND AMERICANS ——————

- Forests cover around 60% of Pennsylvania. Its name means 'Penn's Woods' after its founder, William Penn.

- It has been estimated that at least 33% of blondes in the United States are not natural blondes.

- It is illegal for boys to throw snowballs at trees in Mount Pulaski, Illinois.

- Florida averages the greatest number of shark attacks annually – an average of 13.

- Chinatown in San Francisco is the largest Chinese community outside Asia.

- During World War II, Ellis Island in New York's harbour was a detention centre for illegal or criminal aliens already in the United States. The Coast Guard also trained recruits there. Following the war, fewer people were detained and the facility was closed in 1954. New Jersey has sovereignty over most of Ellis Island.

- While serving in the army at the age of 13, President Andrew Jackson was captured by the British. When the British officer in charge ordered Jackson to clean his boots, Jackson refused and was struck with a sword, leaving a scar on Jackson's face and hand.

—— AMERICA AND AMERICANS ——

- Wisconsin reportedly has the highest proportion of overweight citizens in America.

- During the early days of the Gold Rush in San Francisco, a glass of whisky would cost as much as £3.90.

- Odd place names in Arkansas include Bald Knob, Beaver, Fannie, Hooker, Greasy Corner and Flippin'.

- Across the United States, April is the deadliest month for tornadoes.

- Alaska has more caribou than people.

- Yuma, Arizona, has the most sun of any locale in the United States – it averages sunny skies 332 days a year.

- It is estimated that the average person living in North America opens the fridge 22 times daily.

- There are places in the state of Massachusetts called Ware, Mashpee, Cow Yard and Gay Head.

- Police estimated that 10,000 abandoned, orphaned, and runaway children were roaming the streets of New York City in 1852

———— **AMERICA AND AMERICANS** ————

- In the US, a train crashes into a passenger vehicle every 90 minutes, despite conspicuous warning systems that include flashing lights, blaring bells, and rail-crossing drop-arm barricades.

- Seventy percent of those Americans with a high-school education or less would encourage their daughter if she wanted to be Miss America; 41% of college graduates say they would not encourage her.

- Thomas Jefferson's Vice-President Aaron Burr shot and killed a man in a duel in 1804. Arguing over politics, the men decided on the duel and Burr was charged for murder in New Jersey. However, the state never pursued his conviction on the grounds that 'civilised nations' do not treat duelling deaths as 'common murders'.

- Alaska has a sand desert, with dunes over 100 feet (30 metres) high. It is located along the flatland of the Kobuk River in the north-western part of the state.

- Per capita, it is safer to live in New York City than it is to live in Pine Bluff, Arkansas.

- Each year about $200 million worth of US postage stamps go unlicked. They end up in the albums of stamp collectors, of which there are no fewer than 22 million.

―――――― **AMERICA AND AMERICANS** ――――――

- It is illegal for cars to drip oil on the pavement in Green Bay, Wisconsin. There is a $1 fine for each drip.

- Three US presidents have been the sons of clergymen: Chester Arthur, Grover Cleveland and Woodrow Wilson.

- Alaska is so vast that if you could see one million acres of the state every day, it would take an entire year to see it all.

- Ohio is home to Home, Knockemstiff, Three Legs Town, Ai and Fly.

- Arizona has official state neckwear – the bolo tie. The necktie consists of a piece of cord fastened with an ornamental bar or clasp.

- While serving in Congress, President Thomas Jefferson introduced a bill that attempted to bar slavery from all future states admitted to the Union, a measure that might later have prevented the US Civil War if it had not been defeated – by a single vote.

- Although Mount Everest, at 29,028 ft (8,848 m), is often called the tallest mountain on earth, Mauna Kea, an inactive volcano on the island of Hawaii, is actually taller. Only 13,796 ft (4,205 m) of Mauna Kea stands above sea

AMERICA AND AMERICANS

level, yet it is 33,465 feet (10,200 metres) tall if measured from the ocean floor to its summit.

- Each year, more than 300,000 American teenagers become afflicted with some form of venereal disease.

- Every day in the United States, about a hundred people over the age of 14 commit suicide, a 50% increase in the last decade.

- Each year, approximately 250,000 American husbands are physically attacked and beaten by their wives.

- There are places called Orderville, Plain City and Hurricane in Utah.

- Arizona boasts places called Nothing, Winkleman and Chloride.

- Seventy-three per cent of Americans are willing to wear clothes until the clothes wear out.

- In the United States, a pound (0.45 kg) of potato chips costs 200 times more than a pound of potatoes.

- On average, each American consumes 117 lb (53 kg) of potatoes, 116 lb (52 kg) of beef, 100 lb (45 kg) of fresh

AMERICA AND AMERICANS

vegetables, 81 lb (37 kg) of chicken, 80 lb (36 kg) of fresh fruit, and 286 eggs per year.

● Pittsburgh, Pennsylvania, is the only US city of the nation's largest 50 cities with a higher death rate than birth rate.

● It is illegal to buy ice-cream after 6.00 p.m. in Newark, New Jersey, unless you have a written note from a doctor.

● There are locations in the state of New York called Hicksville, Result and Neversink.

● At 282 ft (86 m) below sea level, Badwater, in Death Valley, is the lowest point in the western hemisphere.

● Chicago, Illinois, was nicknamed the 'Windy City' because of the excessive local bragging that accompanied the Columbian Exhibition of 1893. Chicago has actually been rated as only the 16th breeziest city in America.

● Atlanta, Georgia, began as a small train station in 1837. At that time, it consisted of only a few houses occupied by Western and Atlantic Railroad employees. Since it was the last stop on the railroad line, the 'town' was called Terminus. As the importance of the train station grew and

--------- **AMERICA AND AMERICANS** ---------

the number of employees living in the town increased,
Terminus changed its name in 1843, and was known for
two years as Marthasville. The name changed to the
current Atlanta just a few years prior to the US Civil War,
in 1845. Atlanta was chosen as the 'female form' of
Atlantic to emphasise the city's rail link to the sea.

- There are three times as many households in the
  United States without telephones as there are without
  television sets.

- At least 10,000 years old, the creosote bush in
  California's Mojave Desert is the oldest known living
  thing in the world.

- John Adams was the first president to live in the White
  House – then called the Executive Mansion. He and his
  wife, Abigail, moved into the house in 1800, shortly
  before it was completed. Construction began in 1792.

- Although lobster is regarded as a delicacy today, early
  Americans disliked it so much that they fed it to prison
  inmates several times a week.

- While Jimmy Carter was president, 50 Americans were
  taken hostage by Iran. They were freed the day Ronald
  Reagan, his predecessor, was inaugurated.

———— **AMERICA AND AMERICANS** ————

- Americans spend an estimated £148 billion a year on dining out.

- There are 800,000 dog bites that require medical attention every year. Dog bites rank second behind sexually transmitted diseases as the most costly health problem in the United States. More than 60% of those bitten are children, and 80% of the fatalities are also children.

- Unusual place names in Wisconsin include Spread Eagle, Footville and Ubet.

- Three million cars are abandoned every year in the United States.

- Dogs bite an average of one million Americans a year.

- Odd place names in New Jersey include Love Ladies, Cheesequake and Brick.

- From the 1850s to the 1880s, the most common cause of death among cowboys in the American West was being dragged by a horse while caught in the stirrups.

- Barking Sands Beach, on the Hawaiian island of Kauai, is known for its unusual sand that squeaks or 'barks like a

———— AMERICA AND AMERICANS ————

dog'. The dry sand grains emit an eerie sound when rubbed with bare feet.

- More Americans have died in car accidents than have died in all the wars ever fought by the United States.

- Seattle is considered the best major US city in which to balance work and family.

- Rutherford B Hayes, James A Garfield, Chester Arthur and Benjamin Harrison – who later became presidents – all attended Abraham Lincoln's inauguration.

- Although President George Washington's wife Martha had four children by a previous marriage, the president left no direct descendant. He never sired a child to continue his family line.

- There are places called Drab, Porkey, Virginville, Moon, Mars and Bird-in-Hand in the state of Pennsylvania.

- One school bus ride in Texas is a 179 miles (288 km) round trip.

- About 43 million years ago, the Pacific plate took a north-west turn, creating a bend where new upheavals initiated the Hawaiian Ridge. Major islands formed

———— **AMERICA AND AMERICANS** ————

included Kauai, 5.1 million years old; Maui, 1.3 million years old; and Hawaii, a youngster at only 800,000 years old.

- Odd place names in the state of Mississippi include Chunky, Hot Coffee, Sanatorium, Darling and SoSo.

- Of all the potatoes grown in the United States, only 8% are used to make potato chips.

- Sixteen per cent of Americans say they read the Bible every day.

- Borehole seismometry indicates that the land in Oklahoma moves up and down 25 cm throughout the day, corresponding with the tides. Earth tides are generally about one-third the size of ocean tides.

- It is illegal for frogs to croak after 11.00 p.m. in Memphis, Tennessee.

- Richard Nixon has received more votes than any other person in American history. His three Congressional terms, two terms as Vice-President, his narrow defeat by JFK in the 1960 presidential, his run for the California Gubernatorial, his first election to the Presidency in 1968 and his landslide defeat of George McGovern (the

——— AMERICA AND AMERICANS ———

largest in presidential history until that time) makes Nixon the most-voted-for American politician ever.

- More men than women commit suicide in the United States.

- A whirlpool below Niagara Falls iced over for the first time on record, on 25 March 1955. A huge ice jam in Lake Erie caused more than £3.3 million in property damages near Niagara Falls, New York.

- President Rutherford B Hayes was nicknamed 'His Fraudulency' because he allegedly 'stole' the election of 1876.

- Two out of three adults in the United States have haemorrhoids.

- The most dangerous job in the United States is that of sanitation worker. Firemen and policeman are close second and third places, followed by leather tanners in fourth.

- Wyoming boasts odd place names such as Camel Hump, Big Sandy and Muddy Gap.

- Americans spend approximately £13.8 billion each year on beer.

───── AMERICA AND AMERICANS ─────

- 'Q' is the only letter in the alphabet that does not appear in the name of any US state.

- Thirty-six per cent of Americans say they would not vote an atheist for presidency.

- One of every 11 boxes of cereal sold in the United States is Cheerios.

- Because of San Francisco's rapid recovery from its devastating 1906 earthquake, the city became known universally as 'The city that knows how'. The phrase was originally credited to President William Howard Taft.

- There are locations in the state of South Carolina called North, Coward, Townville and Southern Shops.

- More than 110,000 marriage licences are issued in Las Vegas each year.

- Unalaska, Eek and Deadhorse are places in Alaska.

- Honolulu means 'sheltered harbour'.

- The names of some cities in the United States are the names of other US states. These include Nevada and Louisiana in Missouri, California in Maryland, Oregon

——————— **AMERICA AND AMERICANS** ———————

in Wisconsin, Kansas in Oklahoma, Wyoming in Ohio, Michigan in North Dakota, Delaware in Arkansas, and Indiana in Pennsylvania.

- 'Utah' is from the Navajo word meaning 'upper'.

- Hawaii has the highest percentage of cremations of all other US states, with a 60.6% preference over burial.

- The typical holiday spot for Americans averages 160 miles (257 km) from home.

- There are places in Alabama called Muck City, Burnt Corn and Intercourse.

- California, Arizona, New Mexico, Nevada, Utah, western Colorado and south-western Wyoming comprised the territory taken from Mexico following the Mexican War in 1846.

- Americans consume more than 353 million pounds (about 159 million kilograms) of turkey during National Turkey Lovers' Month in June. By comparison, more than 675 million pounds (about 304 million kilograms) of turkey will be consumed at Thanksgiving.

- A typical American eats 28 pigs in his or her lifetime.

AMERICA AND AMERICANS

- Chicago is home to the world's largest population of Poles outside Warsaw.

- President Thomas Jefferson's father was one of the surveyors who laid out the Virginia/North Carolina border.

- Abraham Lincoln was the tallest president of the US at 6 feet 4 inches (1.9 m).

- The New York phone book had 22 'Hitler' names listed before World War II, and none after.

- Every year, Alaska has about 5,000 earthquakes.

- The states of Washington and Montana still execute prisoners by hanging.

- The most common surname in America is Smith, followed by Johnson and Williams.

- It is illegal to read comics while riding in a car in Norman, Oklahoma.

- Fried chicken is the most popular meal ordered in sit-down restaurants in the US. The next in popularity are: roast beef, spaghetti, turkey, baked ham, and fried shrimp.

──── AMERICA AND AMERICANS ────

- One out of every 15 American adults under the age of 45 got his or her first job with McDonald's.

- Someone dies in a fire every 147 minutes in the United States.

- President Benjamin Franklin devised the first wet-suit for divers, as well as a primitive version of today's flippers.

- President Eisenhower, an avid golfer, had a putting green installed on the White House lawn and had squirrels banished from the grounds because they were ruining the green.

- Nearly 70% of American school students say pizza is their favourite entrée, corn their favourite vegetable, and cookies their favourite dessert.

- In North Carolina, in 1980, a library forbade children to read the Holy Bible without parental consent.

- Twenty-five per cent of Americans believe that Sherlock Holmes was a real person.

- In the US, murder is committed most frequently in August and least frequently in February.

——— AMERICA AND AMERICANS ———

- Americans collectively eat 100 lb (45 kg) of chocolate every second.

- There are more female than male millionaires in the United States.

- President Franklin D Roosevelt's three favourite foods were frog legs, pig knuckles and scrambled eggs.

- Each year 96 billion pounds (about 43 billion kilograms) of food is wasted in the US.

- In Oblong, Illinois, it is punishable by law to make love while hunting or fishing on your wedding day.

- To avoid long encounters with the press, President Ronald Reagan often took reporters' questions with his helicopter roaring in the background.

- On New Year's Day, 1907, President Theodore Roosevelt shook hands with 8,513 people.

- One out of every 11 workers in North Carolina depends on tobacco for their livelihood.

- Nearly 10% of American households dress their pets in Halloween costumes.

AMERICA AND AMERICANS

- In West Virginia, if you run over an animal, you can legally take it home and cook it for dinner.

- Thomas Jefferson wrote his own epitaph without mentioning that he was US President.

- In Florida, it is illegal to sing in a public place while attired in a swimsuit.

- In Connersville, Wisconsin, no man shall shoot off a gun while his female partner is having a sexual orgasm.

- Las Vegas has the most hotel rooms of any city in the world.

- When the diets of inmates of a Virginia juvenile detention centre were changed from typical American junk food to natural foods – cereal without sugar, fruit juice instead of soda, and so on – the number of chronic offenders decreased by 56% and those who were well mannered increased by 71%.

- New Jersey was originally called Albania.

- The US has more bagpipe bands than Scotland does.

- In Dallas, in 1958, fish poured down from a seemingly empty sky. The fish were 3–4 inches (8–10 cm) long and

AMERICA AND AMERICANS

dark grey, with gold specks and red tails. There were no other types of fish or freshwater creatures with them, rendering it unlikely that a tornado had picked up the contents of a river or lake and dropped them on Dallas.

- Until 1857, any foreign coins made of precious metal were legal tender in the United States.

- When the Prince of Wales went to visit the White House in 1860, so many guests went with him, it is said that President James Buchanan slept in the hallway.

- In 1987, American Airlines saved £23,000 by eliminating one olive from its First Class salads.
- Second Street is the most common street name in the US, but First Street is only the sixth.

- Less than one-third of the meals eaten in America are served to the whole family at once.

- In Nebraska, it is illegal for bar owners to sell beer unless they are simultaneously brewing a kettle of soup.

- First-cousin marriages are legal in Utah, so long as both parties are 65 or older.

- Gerald Ford was the only president to have two women

────────── **AMERICA AND AMERICANS** ──────────

attempt to assassinate him. Both attempts were in California in September 1975. The first attempt was on 6 September 1975, by Lynette Fromme, who thought she could impress Charles Manson by killing the president. The next attempt was by Sara Jane Moore, on 22 September 1975. Her motive was simply that she was bored.

- There are 18 doctors in the US called Dr Doctor, and one called Dr Surgeon.

- Three million people in the United States have an impairment of the back or limbs that is a direct result of an accidental fall.

- It takes 15 to 20 minutes to walk once around the Pentagon.

- One American in every 16 will have one of the top 12 most common surnames.

- The average American family spends £228.63 per year on pizza.

- The top of the Empire State Building flexes back and forth a few feet in heavy winds, as the building was designed so that airships could moor at the top.

AMERICA AND AMERICANS

- The banjo is America's only native musical instrument. It was first developed in the south in the 1790s.

- There is a 6-foot-tall (1.8 m) stone monument dedicated to the cartoon character Popeye in Crystal City, Texas.

- Americans use enough toilet paper in one day to wrap around the world nine times. If it were on one giant roll, you would be unrolling it at the rate of 7,600 mph – roughly Mach 10, ten times the speed of sound.

- In New York City, there are 37 taxi drivers who are each named Amarjit Singh.

- President Nixon was known to his fellow college students as 'Iron Butt'.

- The word 'dimes' was originally pronounced 'deems'.

- There is one psychiatrist or psychologist for every 2,641 Americans.

- The Baby Ruth chocolate bar was named after President Grover Cleveland's baby daughter Ruth.

- Presidents George Washington, John Adams and Thomas Jefferson were all keen marbles players.

―――――― **AMERICA AND AMERICANS** ――――――

- The most popular magazine in America is *TV Guide*.

- Today, only 33% of Americans exercise regularly, and 66% are overweight.

- If all the pizza slices Americans eat in one day came from one giant pizza, it would cover more than 11 football fields.

- There is one vending machine for every 55 Americans.

- Bill Clinton is the only president ever to be elected twice without ever receiving 50% of the popular vote. He had 43% in 1992, and 49% in 1996.

- Nine people per day die in America from accidentally drinking, eating or inhaling something other than food.

- One American supermarket chain waxes their cucumbers and apples with floor polish.

- Five hundred Americans freeze to death every year.

- On the outskirts of the small town of Gold Hill, Oregon, is a place that has baffled both visitors and investigators. Nestled in the forest is the Oregon Vortex and house of mystery. There, bottles roll uphill, broomsticks stand by

—————— AMERICA AND AMERICANS ——————

themselves, and people seem to grow and shrink by changing just a couple of steps. If photographs are taken in the area, mist-like forms and balls of light appear in the picture. A plane flying overhead goes through malfunctions in its instruments, suggesting the vortex travels way beyond the ground, high above the region.

- In Bovina, Mississippi, in 1894, a gopher turtle measuring 6 x 8 inches (15 x 20 cm) fell from the sky during a hailstorm.

- In 1980, the city of Detroit presented Saddam Hussein with a key to the city.

- Indiana's state nickname 'Hoosier' came from a generic southern word, meaning 'bumpkin' or 'backwoodsman'.

18

MISCELLANEOUS

MISCELLANEOUS

- Buttons were first worn on clothes in the 14th Century.

- The chain store Woolworths was originally called the 'Great Five Cent Store'.

- Men run 496 of the top 500 companies in the US.

- February 2nd is Groundhog Day in the United States.

- Methuselah was a character in the Bible, but in modern times Methuselahs are containers for champagne.

- Since 1976, there have been over 700 executions in the United States.

- In the Far East, rhino horns are used in medicine.

- The U.S has more than twice the amount of mothers under the age of twenty than Canada.

- There are men in Guam whose full-time job is to travel the countryside and deflower young virgins, who pay for the privilege of having sex for the first time, as it is forbidden for virgins to marry.

- America, black women are four times more likely than white women to die while giving birth.

MISCELLANEOUS

- 38 U.S. states have the death penalty.

- In the United States, February 7th is National Hangover Awareness Day.

- The thirteenth of the month falls on Friday more often than on any other day of the week. In a 400-year period, there will be 688 Friday the thirteenths.

- Christian Dior launched the 'New Look', with its small waist and full skirt in the 1940s.

- Men are four times more likely to attempt suicide than women.

- The coracle boat is made from a wickerwork frame covered with a leather skin.

- The American equivalent of English fashion's 'Sloane Rangers', are 'the Preppies'.

- Among the top twenty industrialized nations, America has the lowest voter turnout.

- 45.5 percent of all murders occur as the direct result of arguments, notably arguments between family members and friends.

MISCELLANEOUS

- Nearly one third of all U.S. executions since 1976 were in Texas.

- 70 of the 3,700 death row inmates in the U.S are minors, or were when they committed their crime.

- John Holmes, a 1970s porn star, had a penis that measured 13.5 inches long.

- Men are more likely than women to carry sexually transmitted diseases.

- In 1978, Ralph Lauren created the 'prairie look' with denim skirts worn over white petticoats

- Ten books on a shelf can be arranged in 3,628,800 different ways.

- Bright yellow and bright blue are the safest and most visible colours for cars.

- Nearly 100 per cent of the dirt in the average home originated from outside – 80 per cent of that comes in on people, stuck to their clothes and their feet.

- The odds against a person being struck by a celestial stone—a meteorite—are 10 trillion to one.

MISCELLANEOUS

- The world's most valuable Barbie doll is the 40th Anniversary De Beers customized doll that was worth £455,000 and wore 22 carat diamonds. At around £10,000 the second most valuable Barbie is an original prototype. Next, if in mint or never-removed-from-box condition, is a brunette 1959 ponytail Barbie that may reach up to £5250.

- The odds against flipping a coin head's up 10 times in a row are 1,023 to 1.

- On average, more animals are killed by motorists than by hunters with guns.

- Monday is the favoured day for people to commit suicide.

- The odds against hitting the jackpot on a slot machine are 889 to 1.

- Deep-sea diving from oilrigs is among the world's most hazardous occupations, averaging a death rate of 1 out of every 100 workers each year.

- The manuals used for launching the first space shuttle would, if all the copies were piled on one another, reach almost twice the height of Chicago's Sears Tower.

MISCELLANEOUS

- Virgin Atlantic discovered that it takes in an average of ten pence per passenger per flight in loose change found in the plane's seats. If that figure holds for the approximate 320 million people who fly from one country to another worldwide each year the total is about £32 million. Lost coins on domestic flights don't amount to much, however. Chicago O'Hare cleaning crews said they found only about three pence per flight. It is suggested that more travellers to other countries 'accidentally' leave foreign coins behind to avoid dealing with them once they get home.

- Car accidents rise 10% during the first week of daylight saving time.

- Half of all murders are committed with handguns.

- Bright yellow and bright blue are the most visible, and therefore most safe, colours for cars.

- There are 48 teaspoons in a cup: three teaspoons make a tablespoon and 16 tablespoons make a cup.

- The odds of someone winning a lottery twice in four months is about one in 17 Trillion. But Evelyn Marie Adams won the New Jersey lottery in this period during 1985–86.

MISCELLANEOUS

- About 66 percent of all traffic death rates occur at night. It is believed that more fatalities occur at night because of more people driving under the influence, even though there are fewer cars on the road than during the day.

- There are more than 200 different types of Barbie doll.

- Every time you lick a stamp, you're consuming one tenth of a calorie.

- 69 percent of accidents occur within 25 miles of home.

- Money isn't made out of paper; it's made out of cotton.

- Most car horns honk in the key of 'F'.

- Some toothpaste and makeup contain crushed volcanic stone.

- University studies show that the principal reason to lie is to avoid punishment.

- The colour combination with the strongest visual impact is black on yellow.

- The popular Barbie doll was without a belly button until the year 2000.

MISCELLANEOUS

- Tablecloths were originally used as towels with which dinner guests could wipe their hands and faces after eating.

- The name of the camel on the Camel cigarettes pack is Old Joe.

- It takes 15 months of instruction at the Pentagon's School of Music to turn out a bandleader, but merely 13 months to train a jet pilot.

- Whether or not you are relaxed or braced during a car accident makes little difference to the severity of your injuries.

- The distinctive smell that you experience upon opening a box of crayons comes from stearic acid, which is the formal name for processed beef fat.

- The art of map making is older than the art of writing.

- Crayola crayons come in 120 colours: 23 reds, 20 greens, 19 blues, 16 purples, 14 oranges, 11 browns, eight yellows, two greys, two coppers, two blacks, one gold, one silver and one white. In early 2001, U.S. President George W. Bush voted for his favourite colour – blue bell. Teen pop star Britney Spears chose robin's egg blue.

MISCELLANEOUS

- The world's most valuable coin was the Sultan of Muscat 1804 Silver Dollar, which sold for $4.14 million dollars at a New York City auction because of its condition and its rarity. The coin is thought to be one of 8 silver dollars presented as proofs to the Sultan of Muscat in 1835.

- It takes the same amount of time to age a cigar as wine.

- The 'sad' emoticon':-(' gets the same trademark protection as a corporate logo or other similar intellectual property. The mark is owned by Despair – an 'anti-motivational' company that sells humorous posters about futility, failure and repression to 'pessimists, losers and underachievers.'

19

LAST WORDS

—————— LAST WORDS ——————

- 'I don't know.'
  Peter Abelard, philosopher

- 'Is it not meningitis?'
  Writer Louisa M Alcott

- 'I am sweeping through the gates, washed by the blood of the lamb.'
  Tsar Alexander II

- 'There are no more other worlds to conquer!'
  Alexander the Great

- 'Give the boys a holiday.'
  Philosopher and scientist Anaxagoras, referring to the school he ran

- 'I see my God. He calls me to Him.'
  St Anthony of Padua

- 'Pardonnez-moi, monsieur.'
  Queen of France Marie Antoinette, after accidentally stepping on the foot of her executioner as she approached the guillotine

- 'For the name of Jesus and the protection of the Church, I am ready to embrace death.'
  Martyr St Thomas à Becket

LAST WORDS

- 'Wait 'til I have finished my problem!'
  Archimedes of Syracuse, mathematician

- 'The ladies have to go first … Get in the lifeboat, to please me … Goodbye, dearie. I'll see you later.'
  John Jacob Astor IV, the richest man in the world, saying farewell to his lover as he gave up his seat on an escaping lifeboat from the sinking Titanic *for a female passenger*

- 'Am I dying or is this my birthday?'
  Lady Nancy Witcher Langhorne Astor, the first female Member of Parliament, in response to being surrounded by her family on her deathbed

- 'Don't worry, be happy.'
  Indian guru Meher Baba, whose last words in 1925 were followed by 44 years of silence before his death in 1969

- 'How were the circus receipts in Madison Square Gardens?'
  Phineas Taylor Barnum, US showman

- 'Ah, that tastes nice. Thank you.'
  Composer Johannes Brahms

- 'Are you happy? I'm happy.'
  American actress Ethel Barrymore (Blyth)

LAST WORDS

- 'Oh, I am not going to die, am I? He will not separate us, we have been so happy.'
  Charlotte Brontë, speaking to her husband of nine months, Reverend Arthur Nicholls

- 'Beautiful.'
  Poet Elizabeth Barrett Browning, in reply to her husband who had asked how she felt

- 'Now comes the mystery.'
  Evangelist Henry Ward Beecher

- 'Friends applaud, the comedy is over.'
  Composer Ludwig van Beethoven

- 'Bless you, Sister. May all your sons be bishops.'
  Brendan Behan, Irish playwright and member of the IRA

- 'What's this?'
  American composer Leonard Bernstein

- 'Who is it?'
  Outlaw Billy the Kid as he was tracked and cornered by Sheriff Pat Garret

- 'Mine eyes desire thee only. Farewell.'
  Catherine of Aragon, first wife of Henry VIII

LAST WORDS

- 'I am about to – or I am going to – die: either expression is correct.'
  Dominique Bouhours, French grammarian

- 'Don't let the awkward squad fire over my grave.'
  Poet Robert Burns, referring to the military recruits who were not yet sufficiently drilled to take their place among the regulars

- 'How gratifying!'
  Poet Robert Browning

- 'Do you know where I can get any shit?'
  US comic Lenny Bruce, who later died of an overdose

- 'Now I am master of myself.'
  Marcus Porcius Cato (the Younger), committing suicide after Julius Caesar's victory over Pompey at Thapsus

- 'Never forget it; decay is inherent in all things.'
  The Buddha

- 'Good night.'
  Poet Lord Byron

- 'And so I leave this world, where the heart must either break or turn to lead.'
  French writer Nicholas-Sebastien Chamfort, in his suicide note

LAST WORDS

- 'All I want to say is I'm innocent. I'm here on a framed-up case. Give my love to my family and everything.'
  Louis Buchalter, the highest-ranking member of organised crime ever to be executed

- 'Stay for the sign.'
  King Charles I, warning his executioner to wait for his cue to behead him

- 'Don't let poor Nelly starve.'
  Charles II, in reference to his mistress Nell Gwynne

- 'I hope never again to commit a mortal sin, not even a venial one, if I can help it.'
  Charles VII of France

- 'Why not? After all, it belongs to him.'
  Charlie Chaplin, in response to the priest who, attending his deathbed, said 'May the Lord have mercy on your soul.'

- 'It's been a long time since I've had champagne.'
  Russian playwright Anton Chekhov

- 'Tell the mayor I'm sorry to be causing the city so much trouble.'
  US murderer Frederick W Cowan, speaking into a telephone before shooting himself

————————— **LAST WORDS** —————————

- 'The sleep of the tomb will press on my eyelid.'
  French poet and political journalist Andre Chenier, guillotined in 1794

- 'Take a step forward, lads. It will be easier that way.'
  Irish patriot Erskine Childers, executed by firing squad

- 'I'm bored with it all.'
  Winston Churchill, before slipping into a coma

- 'Damn it… Don't you dare ask God to help me.'
  Movie star Joan Crawford, speaking to her housekeeper, who had begun to pray aloud

- 'So here it is!'
  Cleopatra, the 'it' being the small asp that she allowed to bite her

- 'Let's forget about it and play high five. I wish Johnny would come.'
  Wild West icon Buffalo Bill Cody

- 'Doctor, do you think it could have been the sausage?'
  French poet, playwright and diplomat Paul Claudel

- 'You sons of bitches. Give my love to Mother.'
  American bank robber and murderer Francis 'Two-Gun' Crowley, before being electrocuted

LAST WORDS

- 'I am not sorry.'
  US President William McKinley's assassin Leon Czolgosz

- 'I'm bored. I'm bored.'
  Gabriele D'Annunzo, Italian poet, novelist, playwright, playboy, war hero, and fascist adventurer

- 'Show my head to the people. It is worth seeing.'
  Georges Jacques Danton, the acknowledged leader of the French Revolution

- 'KHAQQ calling Itasca. We must be on you, but cannot see you. Gas is running low.'
  Aviator Amelia Earhart, whose plane wreck was never found

- 'Carry my bones before you on your march, for the rebels will not be able to endure the sight of me, alive or dead.'
  Edward I

- 'I am not the least afraid to die.'
  British naturalist Charles Darwin

- 'Too late for fruit, too soon for flowers.'
  English writer Walter De la Mare

- 'I'd hate to die twice. It's so boring.'
  Richard Feynman, physicist

LAST WORDS

- 'Swain, can't you stop this (pain)? Swain!'
  Twentieth President of the United States James A Garfield, calling to his doctors who couldn't locate the bullet after he was shot

- 'All my possessions for a moment of time.'
  Elizabeth I

- 'Remember, the death penalty is murder.'
  Wrongfully convicted murderer Robert Drew, executed by lethal injection

- 'Farewell, my friends. I go to glory.'
  Contemporary dancer Isadora Duncan, upon entering the car whose rear wheel would catch her trademark long scarf and break her neck

- 'Yes, I have heard of it. I am very glad.'
  Edward VII, upon being told by his son that one of the king's horses, Witch of the Air, had won the 4.15 race at Kempton Park

- 'This is the happiest moment of my life.'
  German anarchist Adolf Fischer, before he was hanged for his crimes

- 'Watch out, please.'
  Viennese author, critic and theatre director Egon Friedell, whose opposition to the Nazis led to him jumping to his death from an office window, to avoid capture from the Gestapo

LAST WORDS

- 'Who the hell tipped you off? I'm Floyd all right. You've got me this time.'
  US bank robber Charles 'Pretty Boy' Floyd

- 'I love you.'
  Convicted murderer Sean Flanaghan, speaking to his executioner

- 'People want to know if I still love Martha. But of course I do. I want to shout it out. I love Martha. What do the public know about love?'
  'Lonely Hearts Killer' Raymond Fernandez handed this note to a guard as he walked to the electric chair. His lover and accomplice, Martha Beck, had died only a few minutes before

- 'I've had a hell of a lot of fun and I've enjoyed every minute of it.'
  Hollywood movie star Errol Flynn

- 'A dying man can do nothing easy.'
  US President Benjamin Franklin

- 'No, not quite naked. I shall have my uniform on.'
  Frederick William I, King of Prussia

- 'Why fear death? Death is only a beautiful adventure.'
  Pre-eminent American theatrical director Charles Frohman. The phrase was replicated in J M Barrie's Peter Pan

———— **LAST WORDS** ————

- 'I'd like to thank my family for loving me and taking care of me. And the rest of the world can kiss my ass.'
Convicted nun murderer Johnny Frank Garrett, upon being executed

- 'It is nothing. It is nothing.'
Austrian heir to the throne Archduke Franz Ferdinand, on his mortal gunshot wound

- 'Southerly gales, squalls, lee rail under water, wet bunks, hard tack, bully beef, wish you were here – instead of me!'
Global traveller and adventure writer Richard Halliburton's final signal before his vessel disappeared in a storm

- 'Dying is easy. Comedy is difficult.'
Oscar-winning British actor Edmund Gwenn

- 'You promised me that you would help me when I could no longer carry on. Tell Anna about our little talk.'
Austrian neurologist and psychotherapist Sigmund Freud, reminding his friend Dr Schur of his agreement to carry out a mercy killing. Schur gave Freud a little opium, and he died two days later

- 'That's good. Go on. Read some more.'
Twenty-ninth US President Warren G Harding, commenting on some favourable editorials his wife was reading to him when he died suddenly of a heart attack

—— LAST WORDS ——

● 'Let not my end disarm you, and on no account weep or keen for me, let the enemy be warned of my death.'
Genghis Khan, King of the Mongols

● 'Wally, what is this? It is death, my boy. They have deceived me!'
George IV

● 'I came here to die, not to make a speech.'
US outlaw Crawford 'Cherokee Bill' Goldsby, prior to being hanged

● 'My friend, the artery ceases to beat.'
Swiss physician, scientist and poet Albrecht von Haller

● 'I have loved justice and hated iniquity: therefore I die in exile.'
Pope Gregory VII

● 'All is lost. Monks, monks, monks!'
King Henry VIII

● 'Now let the world go as it will; I care for nothing more.'
King Henry II

● 'God will pardon me, that's his line of work.'
Poet Heinrich Heine

LAST WORDS

- 'Open the second shutter so that more light may come in.'
  German writer Johann Wolfgang von Goethe

- 'I know you have come to kill me. Shoot, coward. You are only going to kill a man.'
  Ernesto 'Che' Guevara, Cuban revolutionary leader

- 'I only regret that I have but one life to lose for my country.'
  US revolutionary Nathan Hale

- 'Let us now relieve the Romans of their fears by the death of a feeble old man.'
  Hannibal, Carthaginian military leader

- 'Let's see if this will do it.'
  Actor Jon Erik Hexum as he shot himself with a blank-loaded pistol on the set of TV spy show Cover Up. *The concussion forced a chunk of his skull into his brain; he died six days later, an accidental suicide*

- 'Hold the cross high so I may see it through the flames!'
  Joan of Arc as she burned at the stake

- 'I see black light.'
  French literary legend Victor Hugo

LAST WORDS

- 'Leave the shower curtain on the inside of the tub.'
  Hotelier Conrad N Hilton's response, upon being asked for any words of wisdom

- 'I am about to take my last voyage, a great leap in the dark.'
  Thomas Hobbes, writer

- 'I'm tired of fighting! I guess this thing is going to get me.'
  Legendary magician Harry Houdini

- 'Does nobody understand?'
  Irish novelist and poet James Joyce

- 'Kill me, or else you are a murderer!'
  Jewish-Czech writer Franz Kafka, speaking to his physician, whom he begged to end his pain

- 'On the contrary.'
  Norwegian playwright Henrik Ibsen, upon hearing his nurse inform a visitor that he was feeling better

- 'That is indeed very good. I shall have to repeat that on the Golden Floor!'
  Poet A E Housman, speaking to his doctor, who told him a joke just before he died

LAST WORDS

- 'The prettier. Now fight for it.'
  English playwright Henry Arthur Jones, upon being asked who he would prefer to have at his side during the evening between his nurse and his niece

- 'And now, in keeping with Channel 40's policy of always bringing you the latest in blood and guts, in living colour, you're about to see another first – an attempted suicide.'
  American newscaster Chris Hubbock, before killing herself during a live broadcast in Florida

- 'It came with a lass and it will go with a lass.'
  James V of Scotland, referring to the Crown of Scotland as his only child, Mary, was only six days old

- 'Don't worry, it's not loaded.'
  Rock group Chicago's Terry Kath, playing Russian roulette

- 'I wish I'd drunk more champagne.'
  Economist John Maynard Keynes

- 'Mind your own business.'
  Artist Wyndham Lewis, speaking to his nurse, who had asked about the state of his bowels on his deathbed

- 'Such is life.'
  Australian outlaw Ned Kelly, executed by hanging

———— LAST WORDS ————

- 'That's obvious.'
  John F Kennedy, in reply to the comment of the Texas governor's wife, 'Mr President, you can't say that Dallas doesn't love you.'

- 'My dear, before you kiss me goodbye, fix your hair. It's a mess.'
  George Kelly, American playwright and uncle of Grace Kelly

- 'I'll be in hell before you start breakfast, boys! Let her rip!'
  US train robber Thomas 'Black Jack' Ketchum, whose head came flying off as he reached the end of his rope when hanged

- 'No one can be more willing to send me out of life than I am desirous to go.'
  Bishop Hugh Laud, executed because of his support of Charles I and his opposition to Parliament

- 'Why do you weep? Did you think I was immortal?'
  King Louis XIV of France

- 'Why not? Why not? Why not? Why not? Yeah.'
  LSD guru Timothy Leary

- 'Turn me. I am roasted on one side.'
  St Lawrence as he lay tied face down on a gridiron suspended over a bed of coals, and slowly burned to death

LAST WORDS

- 'They won't think anything about it.'
  Abraham Lincoln, reassuring his wife that it would be all right to hold hands just before John Wilkes Booth sneaked into his theatre box and shot him from behind

- 'They tried to get me – I got them first!'
  Poet Vachel Lindsay, before suicide by drinking Lysol

- 'I wonder why he shot me.'
  Democrat politician Huey P Long Jnr., upon being hit by the son-in-law of a former political opponent

- 'I deserve this fate. It is a debt I owe for a wild and reckless life. So long, everybody!'
  Convicted murderer William P Longley

- 'Is this dying? Is this all? Is this what I feared when I prayed against a hard death? Oh, I can bear this! I can bear this!'
  Cotton Mather, New England minister and Puritan preacher

- 'Shoot straight, you bastards! Don't make a mess of it!'
  Australian Anglo-Boer War soldier and poet Lt Henry H Morant, speaking to the firing squad that executed him

- 'Frenchmen, I die guiltless of the countless crimes imputed to me. Pray God my blood fall not on France!'
  King Louis XVI

LAST WORDS

- 'No, but comfortable enough to die.'
  Maria Theresa, Empress of Austria, speaking to her son Joseph, who attempted to comfort her saying, 'Your Majesty cannot be comfortable like that.'

- 'It has all been most interesting.'
  Lady Mary Wortley Montagu, English writer and world traveller

- 'I am a Queen, but I have not the power to move my arms.'
  Queen Louise of Prussia

- 'Let's cool it, brothers...'
  American political activist Malcolm X, speaking to his three assassins, who shot him 16 times

- 'Dying is a very dull and dreary affair. And my advice to you is to have nothing whatever to do with it.'
  British dramatist and novelist Somerset Maugham

- 'Go on, get out! Last words are for fools who haven't said enough!'
  German political philosopher and economist Karl Marx, in response to his housekeeper who asked if he had any last words

- 'My soul I resign to God, my body to the earth, my worldly goods to my next of kin.'
  Michelangelo, Italian sculptor, painter, architect and poet

LAST WORDS

- 'You will find the word "Calais" written on my heart.'
  Queen Mary I

- 'Hold your tongue! Your wretched chatter disgusts me.'
  French minister Malesherbes, speaking to his priest uttering last rites

- 'My Lord, why do you not go on? I am not afraid to die.'
  Queen Mary II, speaking to Archbishop Tillotson, who had paused while reading a prayer for the dying

- 'Why should I talk to you? I've just been talking to your boss.'
  US writer and gambler Wilson Mizner as he briefly awoke to find a priest standing over him

- 'Last of all, we must die.'
  St Phillip Neri, at the end of a long day seeing visitors

- 'This hath not offended the king.'
  British scholar and statesman Sir Thomas More

- 'I don't want to survive myself.'
  French writer Guy de Maupassant

- 'Tomorrow, I shall no longer be here.'
  Cryptic prophet Nostradamus

LAST WORDS

- 'Human life is limited; but I would like to live forever.'
  Right-wing Japanese writer Mishima Yukio who killed himself after failing to convince the Japanese military to overthrow the civilian government

- 'We are all going.'
  Assassinated US President William B McKinley, responding to his wife as she cried, 'I want to go too, I want to go too!'

- 'Shoot me in the chest!'
  Italian Fascist statesman and Prime Minister Benito Mussolini, speaking to his executioners

- 'I do not have to forgive my enemies. I have had them all shot.'
  Spanish Prime Minister Ramon Maria Narvaez

- 'I don't know what I may seem to the world. But to myself I seem to have been only like a boy playing on the sea-shore and diverting myself in now and then finding a smoother pebble or prettier shell than ordinary, whilst the great ocean of truth lay all undiscovered before me.'
  Sir Isaac Newton, scientist and mathematician

- 'You'll have to drive. I'm hit.'
  Mobster George Nelson, aka Lester Gillis or Babyface, hit by 17 bullets while on the run

LAST WORDS

- 'What an artist the world is losing in me!'
  Nero, Roman emperor

- 'I am just going outside and may be some time.'
  Member of the ill-fated Scott Antarctic expedition Lawrence Oates, walking out of the tent, and vanishing into a blizzard so that his companions wouldn't be hindered by his lameness

- 'Born in a hotel room – and God damn it – died in a hotel room.'
  American dramatist Eugene O'Neill

- 'You wouldn't hang your own sheriff, would you?'
  Crooked sheriff Henry Plummer, lynched for corruption by the townspeople of Bannock, USA

- 'Hurry it up, you Hoosier bastard. I could hang a dozen men while you're fooling around!'
  US serial killer and rapist Carl Panzram, after spitting in the face of his executioner

- 'Here am I, dying of a hundred good symptoms.'
  Writer Alexander Pope

- 'Die, my dear doctor! That's the last thing I shall do!'
  Lord Henry John Temple Palmerston, British Prime Minister and Liberal politician

—————————— **LAST WORDS** ——————————

● 'If I had two lives to give, I'd give one gladly to save Mrs Suratt. I know that she is innocent and would never die in this way if I hadn't been found in her house. She knew nothing about the conspiracy at all.'
Lincoln assassination conspirator Lewis Paine, speaking about cohort Mary Surratt, executed at the same instant

● 'This isn't Hamlet, you know, it's not meant to go into the bloody ear.'
Actor Laurence Olivier, speaking to his nurse, who spilt water over him while trying to moisten his lips

● 'I'm tired. I'm going back to bed.'
George Reeves, American actor who played Superman on the classic 1950s television series. Angry that visitors had awakened him, he announced that he was going back to bed. Instead he went to his bedroom and shot himself in the head with a 30-calibre Luger

● 'Goodbye … Why am I haemorrhaging?'
Russian poet and writer Boris Pasternak

● 'Dear World. I am leaving you because I am bored. I feel I have lived long enough. I am leaving you with your worries in this sweet cesspool. Good luck.'
Oscar-winning British actor George Sanders before taking an overdose of sleeping pills

LAST WORDS

- 'I will be glad to discuss this proposition with my attorney, and that after I talk with one, we could either discuss it with him or discuss it with my attorney if the attorney thinks it is a wise thing to do, but at the present time I have nothing more to say to you.'
  JFK assassin Lee Harvey Oswald, speaking to Inspector Thomas Kelly of the US Secret Service before being assassinated himself by Jack Ruby

- ''Tis well.'
  The first US president George Washington

- 'I am curious to see what happens in the next world to one who dies unshriven.'
  Italian painter Pietro Perugino, giving his reasons for refusing to see a priest as he lay dying

- 'Bring down the curtain, the farce is played out.'
  French satirist Francois Rabelais

- 'Youth, I forgive thee! Take off his chains, give him 100 shillings and let him go.'
  King Richard I, referring to Bertrand de Gourdon, who had shot him with an arrow at Chalus, precipitating his death

- 'Bury me where the birds will sing over my grave.'
  Alexander Wilson, the father of American ornithology

LAST WORDS

- 'Please don't let me fall.'
  Lincoln assassination conspirator Mary Surratt before she was hanged as the first woman ever executed by the US Government

- 'Why yes, a bullet-proof vest!'
  US criminal James W Rodgers, giving his final request before the firing squad

- 'You can keep the things of bronze and stone and give me one man to remember me just once a year.'
  Writer Damon Runyon

- 'Woe is me, I think I am becoming a god.'
  Roman Emperor Titus Flavius Sabinus Vespasian

- 'So little done, so much to do.'
  Gold and diamond mining millionaire Cecil John Rhodes

- 'Never yet has death been frightened away by screaming.'
  Turkish ruler Tamburlaine

- 'I feel this time they have succeeded. I do not want them to undress me. I want you to undress me.'
  Exile of Stalin's Russia Leon Trotsky, speaking to his wife while preparing for surgery due to wounds from one of Stalin's spies

LAST WORDS

● 'Everybody has got to die, but I have always believed an exception would be made in my case. Now what?'
Pulitzer Prize-winning writer William Saroyan, speaking on the telephone to the Associated Press

● 'I feel certain that I'm going mad again. I feel we can't go through another of those terrible times. And I shan't recover this time. I begin to hear voices.'
British novelist Virginia Woolf's suicide note

● 'The car seems OK ...'
Formula One driver Ayrton Senna, seconds before his steering column broke and his car hit the wall, killing him

● 'Good people, be not hurried. I can wait a little.'
William 'Skitch' Snow, British criminal hanged at the second attempt in 1789, as the rope broke the first time

● 'Hell no! No one ever did anything for me. Why in the hell should I do anything for anyone else?'
Mass murderer Charles Starkweather, when asked to donate his eyes to an eye bank

● 'Even in the valley of the shadow of death, two and two do not make six.'
Russian writer Leo Tolstoy as he rejected his friend's pleas to reconcile with the Orthodox Church

LAST WORDS

- 'They couldn't hit an elephant at this dist—'
  General John Sedgwick, mocking the Confederate soldiers in the Army of the Potomac during the American Civil War

- 'Crito, I owe a cock to Asclepius. Will you remember to pay the debt?'
  Socrates, ancient Athenian philosopher

- 'Don't let it end like this. Tell them I said something.'
  Mexican bandit, revolutionary and folk hero Francisco 'Pancho' Villa, speaking to newspaper reporters as he was assassinated by supporters of his enemy

- 'Had I but served God as diligently as I have served the King, He would have not given me over in my grey hairs.'
  Cardinal Thomas Wolsey, English prelate and statesman

- 'Tell mother, tell mother, I died for my country... Useless ... useless...'
  Abraham Lincoln's murderer John Wilkes Booth

- 'Curtain! Fast music! Lights! Ready for the last finale! Great! The show looks good. The show looks good.'
  Broadway producer Florenz Ziegfeld, hallucinating that he was directing one last show